What Makes People Tick

and Why

The Answers Are in the Face

Naomi R. Tickle

Naomi R. Tickle

New edition to *You Can Read a Face like a Book*

Sketches by Alex Tickle and Susan Cranbourne
Cover design by Darlene Swanson of Van-garde Imagery Inc.
Photo of author by Karina Maria Diaz

Library of Congress Control Number: TX 007153027

ISBN: Hardcover   978-1-4653-9952-6
                Softcover   978-1-4653-9951-9
                Ebook   978-1-4653-9953-3

This book was printed in the United States of America.

This book is a new edition of You Can Read A Face Like A Book.

To order additional copies of this book, contact:
Xlibris Corporation
1-888-795-4274
www.Xlibris.com
Orders@Xlibris.com
104353

CONTENTS

The shape of the forehead indicates if you enjoy working with people, things, or information and if you are impatient or enjoy researching; it also indicates a high imagination and very creative.

ACKNOWLEDGEMENTS

I would like to thank the many people who allowed me to interview them in the course of my research. Their stories gave me a deeper level of understanding about the strengths and challenges within us all, which I hope comes across in this book's pages. I greatly appreciated their contributions.

I am grateful to the late Edward Jones and Robert Whiteside, who laid the foundation for this work. Additionally, thanks to all who have followed their footsteps for their contribution to furthering the study of physiognomy.

Special thanks go to my husband, Andrew, who always is present for me, patiently listening to my constant chatter about my latest insights. This book would not have been possible without him. To my children—Martin, Jane, Antony, and Susan—who have always supported and encouraged me in my work, even when they have heard me talk about the same traits a thousand times. I feel very fortunate to have such an incredible family.

Thank you to the many students and friends who have shared their enthusiasm and support for this work—in particular, to Lorraine Kamisky, Chris Deas, and all the amazing friends and business associates who have promoted my work. Thank you for all your help, inspirational ideas, and referrals. I shall be forever grateful.

Of course, I must also thank you, the readers of this book, for your curiosity, which has led you to want to learn more about yourself and the people you meet. You can make a difference in this world by sharing your newly acquired knowledge with others. The purpose of this book lies not in using face reading to judge people, but in using this knowledge to help you recognize that we are all unique individuals. We all have strengths and challenges. How we choose to master them makes the difference.

FOREWORD

The statement "Knowledge is power" remains as true today as ever. In fact, in what has oft been called the information age, knowledge constitutes actual currency.

For this reason, I invest hundreds of dollars a year on books and tapes and videos that offer me knowledge. I have read everything from Nietzsche to Goethe, Blake to the Bible. Why do I do it? Because I am hungry for information, and every book I read or tape I listen to empowers me. Each one represents an investment in myself. As such, these books and tapes are the best investment I ever could hope to make.

I pride myself on being able to choose the right information to expand my mind, so I am delighted—nay, honored—to pen a few words for the introduction of Naomi Tickle's latest book. I'm delighted not only because Naomi is my friend, but because I get to read the book before it hits the presses and the best seller stands, and I'm honored because the information it contains is extremely valuable in so many ways.

This book is filled with knowledge of the most important nature: It is about you, and the more you can know about yourself, the more you can shape your future into the positive projections that you see in your best mind's eye.

I first spoke with Naomi when she did a face reading for me based on a photograph. Actually, prior to that, she had changed my friend's life with one face reading. He subsequently recommended her to me. I was intrigued. When I rang Naomi in America for more detail on face reading, she was out. I left a message. To be honest, I didn't really expect her to get back to me. Most people, particularly if they are well-known authors, never call back, especially long distance. I was delighted the next day when Naomi did call me back; and not only was she gracious, charming, and patient, she also was extremely generous with her time.

At the time, Naomi didn't know me. She could see no immediate profit in me. (There's an old saying that you should never judge anyone, but if you do, judge them on how they treat people who are of no profit to them.) If I had bought a book from her, it probably would not have even covered the bill for the call. Yet she even offered to give me a free reading from a photograph. That's how I knew she was good and that what she had to offer was important.

When Naomi did my face reading, I am delighted to tell you that it was scarily accurate. I was amazed at how much she could tell about me without even having to meet me in person. The information she read from my face substantiated my strong points, pointed out areas in which I needed to trust more, and helped me isolate parts of myself that still needed work. The reading gave me a positive sense of direction and helped me let go of things that were no longer producing results for me. I was delighted.

In that one reading, I learned enough about myself to help me go further along in my personal journey.

One thing I have learned is that we are an inspired species, endowed with the magical ability to create. We can have anything, be anything, and go anywhere. We are all given numerous gifts when we land on this spinning planet. Once we learn to apply them and how the controls operate, the sky is not the limit. It represents just the first stop in a universal journey, both exciting and attainable.

What Makes People Tick & Why is a wonderful and innovative book by a gifted, generous writer. Wherever you want to go, this book will help get you there. I wholeheartedly recommend it to those with their feet on the ground and their eyes on the stars.

Geoff Thompson
Coventry, England
Author and film director
Voted the number one self-defense author in the world

CHAPTER ONE

OUR INNER BLUEPRINT

We all read faces, and we do so from the moment we meet someone. We search the face for clues that help us get a sense of the person to whom we are speaking. The face serves as the template to our inner blueprint. This blueprint gives us immediate insight about what makes people tick and why. It gives us clues about our own personality, our innate abilities, as well as our talents. A person's unique traits are readily apparent even at birth. You can see them in a newborn's face as easily as if you were looking at the baby's DNA, where you can find the same data, such as music, writing, the designer, more detailed, wants the bottom line, and the historian.

From a face reader's, or personologist viewpoint, we genetically inherit the traits from our parents. However, the home environment and personal circumstances we experience while growing up can provide major influences that support or modify both our positive and negative tendencies.

If you were to look at the photographs of your ancestors (and knew what to look for), you would be able to see which personality traits you had inherited from various sides of your family. After reading this book, line up some old family photographs, and look for some of the similarities in the faces. Start at the top of the head and work downward. Their personality traits, as well as unique talents, will begin to unfold before your eyes. You'll be able to notice how many traits you have in common with your family.

Additionally, an individual may inherit a number of opposing traits, which can be "seen" in the number of differences between one side of a face and the other. In some cases, this can cause huge mood changes. Those of you who experience such perplexing behavior will be glad to know your face holds the answer to why you feel this way (and once you understand this, you'll find ways to help you work through those emotions).

In 1909, Frank Parsons, an engineering professor, first used the term "trait," which in this case refers to the relationship between the structure of the face and innate abilities. He developed his trait-and-factor approach to making career decisions. Parsons defined a trait as the characteristic of an ability required for a job.

Please note, throughout this book, I will use the term "trait," which refers to the physical feature in the face being discussed in that section.

The History

Since the time of Aristotle, scientists and philosophers have been fascinated by the relationship between an individual's physical features and his or her personality, characteristics, and behavior. Physiognomy, the approximately 2,700-year-old study of the face, has intrigued and puzzled scientists for years. The first known face readings were made by the Chinese, who used them for diagnosing medical conditions. Later, the structural indicators of the face were used to determine personality types. This also included predicting a time in a person's life when he or she would reach their greatest potential.

Since that time, there have been several attempts to revive the idea that a relationship exists between physical features and behavior. In the 1930s, Los Angeles judge Edward Jones observed the behavioral patterns of the people who appeared before him in court and compared them to facial features. He became so fascinated by his observations that he dropped his judicial work and researched physiognomy, or face pattern recognition, using works that were published by Johann Lavater and other notable authors on the subject. Using established scientific principles, Jones looked at two hundred different facial features and later narrowed the number down to sixty-eight. His studies included hand and body proportions. His research indicated 88 percent accuracy for personality profiling. His system replaced many of the older methods for "typing" people. Thanks to Judge Jones, this "new" physiognomy became the modern-day scientific approach to reading faces. He later termed this study "personology." Today it is referred to as Face Pattern Recognition.

Fascinated by the differences between one side of a person's face and the other, Jones's studies led him to conclude that numerous differences indicate extreme mood changes. When there are nine or more significant differences that can be identified between the left and right side of the face, these individuals may experience many mood changes. One moment they can be on cloud nine; and the next, they may feel very low or have a sinking feeling or possibly become depressed. These mood changes are often perplexing to the individual. What they experience is the push and pull of the traits. When this occurs, it may take a few hours for their emotions to balance or get back on an even keel.

Additionally, Jones discovered that the greater the structural or personality differences between the parents, the greater the likelihood of the child inheriting those differences, hence the asymmetry in the face.

Jones's contribution to the understanding of human nature, as revealed in the face, took physiognomy to a new level of acceptance, credibility, understanding, and application. He applied the new physiognomy to jury selection, personal development, improving relationships, understanding children, sales, and career assessment. He termed this new study "personology."

In addition to the practical uses of face reading, Jones conducted further studies in San Quentin Prison during the 1940s. Warden Clinton Duffy stated at the time, "Many of our men here have been helped immeasurably by [Edward Jones's] staff. The men were better able to handle their personality challenges and how to manage them. This also included career suggestions that would be useful once they were on release. As George H. Cantrell noted, 'As a psychologist, having spent many years in vocational counseling, we now accomplish in hours better results than we would in days before practicing the principles taught by Jones and his staff. It is my hope that in the future we can broaden the scope of this great work."

In 1943, a study was conducted on the freshman class of the United States Air Force Academy to determine how many men would stay the course. The study predicted outcomes with 97 percent accuracy. They also suggested the types of aircraft the pilots should fly. A man I spoke with later validated this story. He shared with me that his father participated in the study and often mentioned to his son how amazed he was by the accuracy.

Later, Jones met up with newspaper editor Robert Whiteside who was, like many before him, somewhat skeptical about face analysis. However, once he received a consultation from Jones, he quickly became an ardent student and advocate of physiognomy. In the 1960s, Whiteside conducted further research on 1,028 subjects to determine the accuracy of personology for personality profiling, relationship improvement and career assessment. The results indicated 92 percent accuracy for personality profiling, 86 percent of the participants stated the information helped them improve their relationships, and 88 percent stated they were satisfied with the career recommended to them after receiving their face analysis.

Does Face Reading Apply to Other Cultures?

The principles of face reading apply no matter what culture one studies. The one major difference seen from culture to culture exists in the wide-set nature of the eyes. According to optometrists, the spacing between the eyes of people with Asian and African heritage tends to be 10 percent wider than in the Western world. Thus, these differences are taken into account when determining the significance of any feature.

You will find many people with Asian backgrounds have wide-set eyes, which indicates a high degree of tolerance. Now I did not say they are patient. Tolerance means one's ability to put up with situations for a long period of time, and this is determined by the set of the eyes. (Impatience is an irritation in the moment. This tendency is determined by the inward slope of the forehead located at the outer edge of the eyebrows.)

The major difference between personology and other approaches to reading faces lies in the fact that Jones extensively researched each trait and narrowed the number of traits to sixty-eight features and their characteristics. The accuracy rate of 88 percent or higher was based on feedback from thousands of people, and including in-person consultations and profiles made from photographs. Special tools were designed to measure the width of the face, position of the ears, the slope of the forehead the width of the eye, plus other measurements.

SOME YEARS AGO, I RECEIVED A REQUEST TO DO A READING OF AN OLD PHOTOGRAPH OF A GREAT-GRANDPARENT OF A CLIENT. THE CLIENT WANTED THE READING TO BE RECORDED ON AUDIOTAPE, WHICH WE DID. SUBSEQUENTLY, THE TAPE WAS PLAYED AT A FAMILY REUNION. DURING THE PLAYING OF THE TAPE OF MY READING, A YOUNG BOY—A DESCENDANT OF THE PERSON IN THE PHOTO—SAID, "MOM, SHE'S DESCRIBING ME!"

To back up these findings, a team of people, including myself, created a computer program for determining careers based on the facial features. The software matches people's physical features that indicate one's innate abilities, to careers that need these abilities. These profiles are based on the U.S. Department of Labor's Dictionary of Occupational Titles. The publication outlines the abilities needed for specific jobs, such as people skills, communication and organizational skills, also the ability to work with details.

We have recently conducted some blind studies with career counselors, comparing our career suggestions with the more traditional tests. We are finding a good match; and in many cases, according to the feedback from our clients, the career suggestions we offered were a better match. We match up the individual's innate abilities seen in the face with career suggestions and look for an 88 percent or higher match. It validates much of what people already know about themselves and gives them the confidence to move forward. So many of my clients have said it confirmed the career they were already considering. Having changed jobs so many times, they just wanted some confirmation they were going in the right direction this time.

My Own Journey

As a child in England, I was fascinated by what I perceived as a correlation between people's face shapes and their behavior. When I shared these observations with my mother, she said, "Don't be so silly. You're imagining things."

In 1981, my interest, in what I would later learn was called personology, was rekindled when I took a color course with the late Suzanne Caygill, the "grand dame" of the color industry, at the Academy of Color in San Francisco. Suzanne's ability far exceeded any color system developed during or since that time. No one has come close to matching her talent. I found it fascinating to watch her work with her clients; she painted a portrait of them with color swatches, textures, and prints. These reflected and brought out all the qualities seen in the face.

During the training with Suzanne, a man came in for a color analysis. A student of personology (another name for physiognomy), he was looking for volunteers on whom he could practice his new skills. Like many, when I first learned about face reading, I was skeptical because it sounded like another new age pursuit. After listening to my friends and hearing their excitement at having their "charts done," curiosity got the better of me. With some hesitancy, I made an appointment with a personology consultant, making sure no one except my husband knew what I was about to do. To my amazement, the reading was extremely accurate. Plus I immediately saw how the information could significantly contribute to the quality of people's lives.

Since then, there have been many times I have shared a few quick observations with people based on what I see and what I know about personology. Sometimes people think I have some extraordinary psychic or intuitive ability. This is not so. I gather this information purely from looking at the physical structure of the face, including the eyebrows. I only work with the information I have before me. According to the feedback from my clients, they find assessments in person and from photographs extremely accurate. However, even after that first reading, I could immediately see how useful personology would be for high school and college graduates and people in career transition. It provides another tool that can help them get back on track with their lives.

> PERSONOLOGY IS JUST ANOTHER TOOL THAT WILL HELP US BETTER UNDERSTAND OURSELVES AND BE MORE CONSCIOUS OF OUR COMMUNICATION AND INTERACTION WITH OTHERS. IT HELPS US UNDERSTAND OTHERS SO THAT WE CAN LEARN TO LISTEN, RATHER THAN REACT OR MAKE HASTY JUDGMENTS.

From an early age, we innately know our interest. However, our intuitive sense of this often gets smothered through the early school years. Later, as we grow into adults, we are influenced by other people's well-intended advice or comments that often cause us to repress our natural knowingness about ourselves and what we like or don't like. This applies to the career choices we make or the hobbies we enjoy. Have you ever shared with someone what you would really like to do, and they responded, "That sounds boring," "What do you want to do that for?" or "That'll never work" You may have told family members and simply received a clear lack of interest and support on their part.

When we constantly receive non-supportive responses to our interests throughout our lives, we begin to doubt ourselves. We start to internalize other people's opinions and beliefs, and we begin to think that the nonsense they tell us is really true. Then we start to experience inner conflict. Our "learned behavior" and our "natural knowing" battle each other.

Of course, plenty of skeptics are only too eager to jump in and criticize personology. They call personology "new age voodoo," passing judgment without having experienced a personal assessment. They post negative comments on the Internet or cast disapproving remarks at meetings without even researching or testing out the methodology first.

However, real scientific evidence supports the accuracy of personology. One cannot ignore confirmation staring us in the face (no pun intended). Besides, we all read faces anyway and make snap judgments based on how people look. The face is full of information. Why pretend it isn't there for us to clearly view? Are we afraid of what we'll see—or what others will see?

Unlike the skeptics, be willing to explore and test out the information in this book. Keep in mind this constitutes an introduction to reading faces and only discusses the extremes. When the traits are neither high nor low, the person will exhibit both behavioral tendencies. Plus many traits are not included in this book; these traits are covered in advanced studies. However, to do an accurate assessment requires "hands-on" training.

Which Career?

Many people come to me for a career profile because their high school or college students are searching for a career direction. Many of my clients are experiencing frustration with their current job or are in a midlife career change. I have worked with a number of graduate students who are still looking for the ideal career. Having tried many other career evaluation tests, these people are seeking alternative solutions to finding the right career. After they get the results of their career profile, they usually say, "Where were you when I needed you?"

I receive photos from people who live all over the world, and I see clients in person. The feedback from my clients indicates the profiles I give them, after evaluating their faces, are at least 90 percent accurate.

Exploring other areas of aptitude or personal interest only enriches your life's experiences and adds value to the career upon which you finally decide upon. However, according to psychologists, at least 70 percent of the workforce do not enjoy their jobs. Many people in their late forties and fifties state they hate their jobs, but the jobs pay the mortgage and put food on the table. These discontented people count the days to retirement.

Why are people so off track? Parents and teachers have significant influence on the choices students make. Parents want their sons or daughters to follow in their footsteps or to find careers that pay well. Often, artistic pursuits are discouraged, just as they were with the boy in the movie *Billy Elliot*. Billy's father frowned on the idea of his son becoming a dancer. It wasn't a "manly" thing to do. It took some time and determination on the son's part before the father realized how talented and passionate his son was about dancing. He had to let go of his desire for his son *not* to be a dancer. Only then did he let him pursue his true interests.

A young Chinese college student desperately wanted to be an artist. She took some art classes in college. However, her parents thoroughly disapproved and wanted her to become an engineer instead. She followed their wishes. Despite her efforts to enjoy engineering courses, she struggled to get through them. Eventually, an opportunity arose for her to do some illustrations for one of the classes she was taking. Of course, she loved doing the drawings. This presented the turning point in her life. She resumed her artistic studies and went on to become a successful artist and sculptor.

A NOTE TO PARENTS: LISTEN TO YOUR CHILDREN, AND FIND OUT WHAT IGNITES THEIR PASSION. IT IS THEIR LIFE, AND IT IS THEIR DREAM. AS PARENTS, WE NEED TO ALLOW OUR CHILDREN THAT FREEDOM.

You'll Never Look at a Face the Same Way Again

Personology represents a very simple and uncomplicated exercise. What you see is what you get. The traits discussed in this book can easily be determined by simple observation. Does the person have a wide or narrow face? Is the hair fine or coarse? Do they have full or thin lips? Is the nose pointed or rounded?

Specifically designed tools are used for measuring face and head proportions. These tools are not needed for nonprofessional spot analysis, however. To become a qualified expert in the field of personology requires formal training by a qualified personologist. Training programs and workshops are available in the United States and Europe.

This book serves as just the beginning of your education. Far more structural/behavioral patterns exist than those I've describe in these pages. I've attempted to give you enough information so you can start learning more about yourself, discovering what makes you act in certain ways, understanding why you experience certain emotions, and becoming more aware of how you communicate to others—particularly people close to you. You also can begin understanding what makes the people around you tick as well. In this way, you can live closer to the "examined life" that Socrates spoke of centuries ago.

Throughout this book, I will relate real-life stories and responses from people with whom I have worked. I interviewed more than five hundred people, and I have discovered how challenged people can feel when they have some of the traits I describe, particularly when certain traits are in conflict with one another. As you read, study one trait at a time until you have fully mastered the concept.

I should warn you, however; when you have finished reading this book, you will never look at faces in the same way again.

Know Thyself

Understanding your own traits represents the first step toward becoming the individual you want to be. This book does not claim that the knowledge of face reading will allow you to perform miracles, nor does it claim that by using the principles of personology, you will magically transform into a completely fulfilled human being. It does however claim to provide an introductory map to assist you on your personal quest toward an understanding of yourself—not for ultimate answers. This will allow you to learn how to relate and communicate with others more effectively. Learning how to identify the traits in your own face allows you to identify your innate talents and get in touch with who you are, rather than continuing to buy into the belief systems others may have imposed upon you.

In a world where many people spend their lives doing things they hate, personology gives you vital clues about your innate gifts. It's your GPS (global positioning system) acting as a reminder when you drift off course. Simply look at your face to find out where you need to go or what you need to do. For example, the rounded outer rim of the ear indicates a love of music. Individuals with square chins love debate, are good at mediation, or enjoy fighting for a cause. Small lines that flare out from the inner corner of the eye suggest an innate ability to write. The eyebrow that flares upward offers a reminder to go to the theater or take up drama.

Take time out and find a quiet space. Think about the things you enjoy. What thoughts come up? What generates excitement or passion within you? Is it an activity, a favorite place, the aroma of old books, or certain nostalgic buildings brings back the times in the past? What were your dreams as a child? Then look at your face, and find confirmation there, for how you should be spending your time and your energy.

The purpose of this book is to introduce you to some of the well-researched personality traits that will help you gain a better understanding of yourself and people throughout the world. To accomplish this goal, study one trait at a time, and notice how people with certain traits respond to situations or how they behave. The more you are able to understand and apply the concepts discussed in this book, the greater are the chances that it will help you gain amazing insight into human behavior. It will open a new understanding about what makes people tick and why. You will see people throughout the world with a whole new perspective—just by looking at their faces.

Chapter Two

The Applications

Many applications exist for personology including career assessments, sales and marketing, team building, and coaching. Personology also helps individuals who work in the area of human resources, teaching, customer relations, and personal development classes. Additionally, knowledge of personology can improve relationships, including those between parent and child. In particular, it has proved to be very helpful for understanding foster or adopted children.

Careers Choices

Thousands of high school and college students leave school confused by their many career choices. I am told as many as 70 percent have no clue about what direction to take after graduation. They've completed the career and personality assessment tests, have a diploma in hand, but still they are unable to make this decision. If they do have an idea about what they'd like to do, many receive comments from their parents, teachers, and friends that do not support their interests. This usually hinders, rather than helps, their decision-making process.

In fact, many people have expressed how much impact the negative comments they received, which are related to their interests, had on the path they ended up taking. For instance, I suggested to a woman I met at an event that she would have done well in psychology. She responded, "That was a career I really wanted to pursue, but my parents said, 'Why do you want to listen to people's problems all day?'" I also suggested she try teaching. Again, she said her mother had told her, "You'll never make much money in teaching." So this woman was left wondering what she should do with her life. Later, she launched her own business, which proved very successful, but it never really satisfied her. She often wondered what career she should have pursued. Hearing my suggestions validated her earlier interests. I suggested she might want to take up life coaching. It's a shorter course of study than becoming a psychologist or teacher, plus it's very portable; you can practice anywhere. Her eyes lit up at this idea.

Now when I notice certain abilities in a young child's or student's face, I often suggest careers or interests they might want to take up, such as music, writing, a certain sport, or a particular hobby. They respond with amazement and delight when I confirm their interests. For instance, I remember seeing a sixteen-year-old boy in a wheel chair. Noticing he had all of the facial traits for editing or making documentary films, I felt compelled to ask him about his future plans. He shrugged his shoulders and said he didn't really know. I suggested he take up editing or making documentary films. Upon hearing my comment, his mother exclaimed, "I can't believe you said that. Next week, he will pick up the top award for the best documentary film in school."

This young man raised his fists, and with a big smile on his face, he exclaimed, "Yes, I'm on the right track!" I simply connected the abilities I could see in his facial features to careers he might enjoy. I noticed a young man in a garage helping people out with their parking tickets, he had the same traits as the young man in a wheel chair. I felt compelled to ask him if was he going to college, and what were his plans. His response was he was a high school drop out and who would want him. I shared my thoughts, whereupon he took my hands in his and said, "I was at the lowest point in my life today, you have just turned my life around." Film editing had been an area of interest he had thought about.

I JUST GOT YOUR REPORT—WHAT A FANTASTIC THING! THE BOILED-DOWN PART ABOUT CAREERS, AVOCATIONS, AND HOBBIES WAS EXACTLY ON TARGET. II REALLY ENJOYED THE PROCESS. THANKS SO VERY MUCH.

Although one cannot always make such a quick evaluation, some trait combinations are easier to connect than others—with or without a personology profile. During a meeting, I mentioned to those in attendance that if we were to look back over our early years in school, we would see a pattern emerging that would reflect our interests. Elinor, who was at the meeting, mentioned that in fifth grade the students in her class were asked to put together an advertising campaign to promote and sell milk. She put together her campaign, and when the day came to try and actually sell the milk, the longest line formed at her table. Her teacher felt she stole the show and would not allow her to compete again. It turned out she had the highest sales recorded in school that year.

Many years later, when her children were grown, Elinor decided she wanted to go back to work again; her husband suggested she would be good in sales. Within three months of joining a company, despite negative comments from fellow coworkers, she became the top salesperson. Her interest in sales was renewed, and since then, she has written a number of books in which she has shared her many experiences and insights on selling.

I WAS SO ASTOUNDED AND GRATIFIED WHEN I GOT MY CAREER PROFILE. YOU WERE RIGHT ON TARGET!

As one young man shared with me, "I was so astounded and gratified when I got my career profile. You were right on target! You said the first career you thought of for me was film and animation or cartoonist. Well, for the past two years, I've been reading books on screenwriting, and I currently work at an animation TV network! I just finished my first feature film script. About a month before my career assessment, I had even purchased a book on how to draw animated characters. I had thought it might be a fun thing to do in my spare time. I often felt like my interest in screenwriting was just a hopeless pipe dream, so I'm very happy to say that your career assessment gave me hope for the first time in a long time."

Knowledge of personology allows you to make career suggestions. In this book, I will cover some of the traits that indicate innate abilities for certain careers. A match for any given career is indicated by a combination of at least ten abilities. It's not just based on one trait alone.

Relationships

According to published statistics, 60 percent or more marriages fail. Couples get so caught up in the early emotions of the relationship that they blind themselves to the differences that may arise later. This impacts their children, if they have any, tremendously, as does the conflict that comes up during and after the separation process.

Understanding your own traits, and your partner's, represents the first step toward creating a meaningful relationship. Knowing more about each other's traits will not provide miracles, nor will it magically transform your relationship. The information does however provide a map to assist you on your personal quest—not for ultimate answers—but toward an inner understanding of yourself and how to communicate with your partner most effectively. This helps create and support a long lasting relationship.

Learning how to use personology to identify each other's traits will help you better understand and recognize the behavioral tendencies that create challenges within your relationship. People are who they are. Moving in together or getting married does not mean your partner will change his or her ways. The more couples know about the person with whom they are thinking of living with, the better the chances of the relationship working.

HI NAOMI, I AM NOW DATING JACK. YOUR INFORMATION IS IMMENSELY HELPFUL. TO HAVE INSIGHT ON HIS CHARACTER ALLOWS ME TO BE AT PEACE WITH THE DYNAMICS OF OUR FRIENDSHIP.

We all have challenges; how we handle them and the way we communicate will make a significant difference in the quality of our relationships. If you care enough about each other, then be prepared to work out the differences that are bound to come up.

Knowledge of personology can help you through tough times, and it can help you understand yourself and your significant other; thus, assisting you in maintaining a healthy and strong relationship. For example, after Jeffery attended my workshop, he realized, for the first time, how his criticism was impacting his marriage. The day after the workshop he caught himself criticizing his wife and immediately apologized. He became more aware of his critical nature.

I highly recommend that couples contemplating living together or getting married have a Relationship Profile prior to the commitment. This assessment can be made in person or from photographs. It gives couples a "heads up" before making this type of commitment and saves lots of hurt feelings, time, and money. Why go through the pain of trial and error when a small investment may help to smooth out the rough spots or avoid those bumpy times?

Sales and Marketing

Learning how to read key features in the face helps you better understand and work with clients. It removes the roadblocks that sometimes come up when working with other people. For instance, one day while out walking, I saw a family in the park with their three-year-old son. As I passed them, they called for their son, who had wandered off, to come back, but he took no notice of them. As I was about to pass the family for a second time, I noticed the young boy was much further away. His parents were now shouting at him to return, but he was completely ignoring them. As I walked, I found myself near to the boy, so I told him his parents were calling for him to come back. He looked at me defiantly; there was no way he was going to return. Noticing that his head was wider at the back than the front, I immediately knew he had a very competitive nature. So I said to him, "On the count of three, I'll race you back to your parents." At the count of three, he raced back to them without looking back until he was in his father's arms. I never moved one foot. His parents waved to me in appreciation, although they had no idea what I had said to him.

I spoke to that little boy in a way that elicited the most cooperation. Instead of getting resistance, I was able to get results that worked for everyone. This tactic works just as well in sales, marketing, and customer relations. Recognizing an individual's communication style and how to best approach or work with that person removes a lot of stress in the work world. It also helps build client relations. And when you know something about a person's personality traits, it can help you make a sale go more smoothly.

Human Resources

Companies spend millions of dollars trying to hire the right person for a job. Often times, they hire someone only for that person to leave a few months later, or for them to find that they need to let that someone go. Personology gives human resource professionals another tool to use during the interview and decision-making process. You simply match up people's innate abilities with careers or activities they enjoy doing. This does not mean that someone who does not have the right facial features who applies for the job wouldn't be any good at it; with training and determination, they could excel.

I gave a workshop at a college, which was attended by many of the staff, including some of the people who worked in the recruiting office. However, the people who did the hiring for the college were unable to attend. Three weeks later, the people in the recruiting office noticed a new person had been hired as an accountant. They all wondered how long she would last. By looking at her face, they realized the woman did not have the traits needed for a highly detailed job. Sadly, she only lasted three weeks and was fired. Not only was this devastating to the woman, the college wasted money and time hiring the wrong person.

This happens often in thousands of businesses worldwide. Yet an understanding of face analysis put to use by human resource professionals can avoid this problem in many cases. It saves time and money, plus it creates an effective team that works well together.

Children

As a parent, knowing more about your children or your adopted or foster children helps you recognize their innate strengths, challenges, and abilities. This helps parents encourage their children to pursue their interests and abilities. Parents also find it useful for understanding how to best approach and work with their children's most challenging traits. This helps you smooth out or avoid many of the more difficult situations that can arise.

Susan brought in her blind nine-year-old daughter to see me. She attended a special school for children with learning disabilities in Wales, but it required a twice-weekly two-hour journey by bus. After completing her personology profile, mechanical engineering seemed the career most suited for her. I struggled with this choice because of her disability. When I mentioned this to Susan, she told me her daughter loved to take machinery apart and put it together again. In fact, she had good hand dexterity and design and organizing traits. I also mentioned to her mother that she had far above average intelligence, which could be seen in her high forehead. As it turned out, her mother had brought her in to see me because she thought her daughter was very intelligent.

Back at home, a repairman came to fix Susan's washing machine. Her daughter approached him, and said, "It's missing on the first cycle. Will you show me how to fix it?" He was so amazed by her request that he took extra time to explain to her what needed to be done. Susan was fascinated.

After her face analysis session, Susan's daughter grew by leaps and bounds. Personology validated much of what she knew about herself and gave her renewed confidence, which created a huge turning point in her life. Her mother re-enrolled her in a regular school at that point, where she was much happier. Susan shared with me later that her daughter excelled at school and had a whole new level of confidence. In fact, she felt that all children should go through this assessment. It made such a difference to her daughter.

I believe many of the "at-risk" children and teenagers would highly benefit from a personology profile. So often parents, teachers, and counselors look at what is wrong with their children, rather than help them explore their inner potential.

Understanding children's traits from the very beginning helps avoid the challenges that confront parents. In a television interview with youngsters, who had committed various crimes, it became evident that many of them shared a specific trait cluster. They all had the High Self-Confidence (wide face), Competitive (head wider at the back compared with the front), and Forward Balance (more face in front of the ear compared with the back). This does not mean every child or teenager with this trait cluster will get into mischief if one's traits are not channeled. It just provides a "heads up," so parents can be aware should the behavior gets out of control.

Many an adult has shared with me that if only their adopted or biological parents had understood them, it would have made all the difference in their upbringing and their life in general. Knowing something about their children's strengths and challenges gives parents a better understanding of their children, especially adopted or foster children. It helps the parents encourage their child to pursue their natural interests at a young age, rather than discover them years later—or may be never.

It's time for teachers and psychologists to remove the barriers that automatically come up for them when I mention the insights that Personology has to offer. This work could make a significant contribution in understanding students and helping them on their life's journey.

Your Ancestors

When we look at photographs of our ancestors, we often wonder about their lives, and who they were. Once you have mastered personology, you'll be able to identify a few of their traits, and you'll get an idea about their character and possible interests simply by studying those pictures. Make a note about which traits you inherited from them.

I was asked to do an assessment for a family reunion from a photograph of a great-great-grandmother. This included an audio that would be played at the event. As some of the young family members listened to the description of their grandmother, they felt it described them.

Knowledge of reading faces also helps you understand family members. We often hear about the disagreements that come up among siblings or children and parents. In extreme cases, they may never talk to each other again. Knowing more about your family members, will help you understand why they react the way they do, and you will become aware of how your style of communication affects others. It helps overcome differences and heal old relationship wounds.

Diane expressed the sadness she felt about the fact that her daughter never spoke to her anymore. When I identified her controlling trait cluster, which she confirmed, it explained her daughter's reaction. Her daughter thought her mother was trying to control her life and felt very restricted. This affected her life so much that the only way of coping with her controlling mother was to have nothing more to do with her. I suggested she phone her daughter and make amends. At that time, her daughter was not answering any phone calls from her mother. If her daughter would not pick up the phone, I suggested, perhaps, she can ask a family member to set up a meeting. After a short period of time, Diane and her daughter began speaking to each other again.

Character Casting

Another application of personology involves character casting for theater, films, or advertisements. Progressive Insurance Company and Geiko do an excellent job at type casting for their advertisement.

When advertising or theater companies match an actor's facial features to the character for which they are auditioning, it makes the actor or actress come across as more believable in the role they are portraying. In the field of advertising, this increases sales.

Team Building

I have worked with a number of start-up companies. The major players in those companies later shared with me how important a part the face assessments played in helping them launch a successful business. When you put together a team of people who understand how to work together, it avoids much of the wasted time that occurs from miscommunication.

Personology takes less time than other similar methodologies. I worked with some top directors launching a new branding company in England. They asked me to do an individual face assessment for each of them, so they would better understand how to work together as a team. Later, the CEO of the company told me that what I had uncovered within the short time I was with them would have taken his son, who does psychometric testing for companies, months to have discovered. Psychometrics is the study of educational and psychological measurement instruments, such as questionnaires and tests of knowledge, abilities, attitudes, and personality traits.

One company I worked with suggested one of their employees to work in outside sales. When I suggested this person would be more suited to a job behind a computer, the employee felt greatly relieved. She dreaded the idea of sales. She had a flat forehead, which told me she had the trait of a person oriented toward things and information. These individuals are not as social as most people inclined toward sales. They are more information driven.

Many companies send me photographs of people they are considering hiring. Basically, my assessment confirms what they had already decided as far as job compatibility. The major difference between their assessment and mine lies in the fact that I did not know the candidate, nor did I ask them any questions. This reassures the client that they are making the right decision about hiring a person for a particular job. The more information you have about a potential job candidate, the better the decision you can make.

Keep in mind that experience always influences an employer's decision about who to hire. A personology profile just gives employers some additional insight about the candidates applying for the job, no matter what their level of experience is.

The above applications represent just a few of the areas where personology can be applied. In addition, it will help you in business situations or at social events, when meeting someone for the first time, and when dealing with the more challenging people that cross your path. Personology serves as a tool you can take with you no matter where you travel.

On the last day of a cruise, along with many other passengers, I was waiting in line to settle my account. The man behind me was feeling agitated and was giving the crew members a hard time. I thought I needed to deal with the situation since we would be in line together for a while. Turning around, I quickly noticed his very close-set eyes, which indicated that he had the Low Tolerance trait. I immediately knew how to smooth out the situation. I said, "I realize this delay is very frustrating, but we are all in the same boat . . . no pun intended. We just need to be patient, and chances are, it will go more smoothly." He said not another word for the rest of the wait.

With practice and training, you will be able to instantly recognize how to best approach someone and how to smooth out the rough spots.

Please note, throughout the book, I will be discussing the extremes of each trait, which will be referred to as "high" or "low." Everyone has a degree of each trait. For the sake of basic learning, we will just be looking at the opposites or extremes. To determine what degree of a trait someone has, additional training, more than what can be provided in this book, would be required.

CHAPTER THREE

THE ASYMMETRICAL FACE

Mood Swings

The first thing you need to know when learning personology, or how to read a face, is that faces are not symmetrical. The degree of asymmetry in your face indicates to a large extent the amount of mood swings you experience. In other words, how many differences you have in features from one side of your face to the other determine your mood extremes.

To see the difference between the right and left side of your face, first, take your hand and cover the right side of your face, then switch and cover the left side. Notice if you have more face on the left side compared with the right side. Is the corner of one eye closer to the center of the nose than the other? Are your eyebrows the same shape? Does the outside corner of one eye go down and the other up? Are the two center corners of the eye level? These represent some of the more obvious differences commonly found in faces.

I have never recorded more than twenty-three differences in one person's face. A woman I worked with, who had these extreme differences, experienced significant mood changes when her life became out of balance. After the assessment, she became more aware when these mood changes occur and she was able to manage them better. She now understands why she experiences such severe mood swings, and she is able to turn them around when the need arises. Her doctor had diagnosed her as having manic depression. After her profile, she was better able to manage those extreme moments in her life.

Everyone experiences some mood changes. However, the greater the differences between the two sides of the face, the greater the mood swings. As I mentioned earlier, this asymmetry results from the parents' facial structures being significantly different from each other, which in turn indicate that the parents' had extreme opposites in their own personalities. If the child inherits these different behavioral patterns, he or she may appear moody to others when in fact, he or she is just experiencing the push and pull of his or her parents' traits. And the differences between the parents' traits can easily be seen in the asymmetry of the child's face.

When people have these extreme mood swings, they can be all for something one moment, and change their minds in the next. They are enthusiastic about the start of a new day, and suddenly they feel unsure of themselves or feel depressed. These mood changes can sometimes make these individuals unpredictable and complex. When an individual's life is out of balance, the mood changes can last for a few hours or the whole day. The more out of balance a person's life, the greater the mood swings. This can be frustrating and confusing to everyone—to the individual having these experiences, as well as to the people with whom one works and lives with. One client who had these extreme emotions said simply identifying them really helped to explain what set off the mood changes.

Being more aware of the challenges that may come up in relationships improves the communication and a better understanding of each other, especially when dealing with mood changes or the traits that may create challenges. Instead of taking offense, we can gain the knowledge of how best to cope in these situations. A couple of friends decided to go on a sailing trip together. Based solely on my observations of his physical features, I forewarned one of them that his sailing partner could be emotionally explosive at times. I advised him not to take the situation personally when it came up but to find ways to smooth it out. After the trip, my friend expressed the value of having that information prior to the trip. Since he was forewarned, he was prepared when the outbursts occurred. Had he not been prepared for this behavior or suspected that this behavior might occur, it could have ruined the whole trip. They were able to get through the more challenging moments and had a great time. It was even suggested going sailing together again.

Those of you who do not experience these mood changes may find this information strange. Yet many people have broken down when they finally understood the cause of the imbalances in their lives. They had been dealing with the situation for years and never understood why they were so emotionally changeable. Once the reason was identified, they felt a load lifted off their shoulders.

While you can't change your facial structure, and you can't change the traits you inherited, you can find ways to handle the mood swings created by those inherited traits. There are several ways to manage these mood changes. When I experience them, I recognize what is happening and then deliberately find ways to physically move myself through these moments. You might try going for a walk or a bike ride or doing any activity you enjoy that will help you through your mood swings.

Chapter Four

The Eyes Are the Windows of the Soul

Tolerance

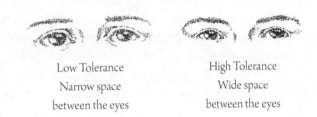

Low Tolerance	High Tolerance
Narrow space	Wide space
between the eyes	between the eyes

The eyes are one of the first features we notice when we meet someone for the first time. From the eyes, we get an immediate sense about whether a person is friendly, intense, laid-back, or easy to get along with.

Tolerance, one of the most important traits, indicates the timing of emotional responses and reactions in the moment. Tolerance has nothing to do with impatience, rather it indicates how long we will put up with a situation before we respond, how much we will let things deviate from the way they should be before we correct them. This trait is determined by the spacing of the eyes. Individuals with close-set eyes react to situations more quickly and want to work by the rules. Wide-set-eyed individuals are extremely tolerant and laid-back.

To accurately determine this trait, start practicing with photographs, making sure the person's face is looking directly at the camera. First, draw a line down the center of the nose, starting between the eyebrows. Second, measure the distance between the eyes from inner corner to inner corner. Third, measure the width of the eyes from inner to outer corner.

If the eyes are the same size as the space between the eyes, this indicates someone who is just tolerant. If the eye measures larger than the space between the eyes, this individual will have extremely low tolerance under pressure. If the width of the eye measures smaller than the space between them, this individual will be a lot more tolerant and work well under pressure.

Low Tolerance: Close-Set Eyes

People with low tolerance tend to focus on the issue at hand. They have an intense "now" reaction, which makes them present in the moment, and a built-in sense of right and wrong. When intent on something, nothing else exists for them. If you need to get their attention, give them some time to break away from what they are doing. This helps avoid irritating them or making them snap at you. These individuals perform better when working on one or two projects at a time; they feel overwhelmed when faced with a number of tasks at once. These people also feel pressured when multitasking and tend to snap at others; then they become hard on themselves for being so intolerant. They don't want to be intolerant. If their daily activities require multitasking, after a while they will adjust. However, they feel a great sense of relief when the pressure to do so goes away.

One of my clients with close-set eyes shared that she criticizes herself when she becomes intolerant because she feels her behavior is inappropriate. She is equally intolerant of other people's behavior; she has a difficult time when people break rules she doesn't allow herself to break. Whereas, an individual with wide-set eyes would be more likely to say, "Relax. Don't worry about it." They would see my client as overreacting to these situations.

Low Tolerance

Many times, in the work world, individuals with close-set eyes find themselves feeling overwhelmed by their responsibilities. If they have very demanding bosses, this adds to their stress. This was very apparent when a man with the Low Tolerance trait came to install our high-speed telephone line. He had thirteen service calls to make that day. He was under extreme pressure, which affected the quality of his work. He was in such a hurry to finish the job that he inadvertently cut off a couple of phone lines.

When you find yourself facing a company or store employee or anyone who comes across as intense, stressed, and "in-your-face," don't take it personally. If they have close-set eyes, find ways to relax them. When I was renewing my driver's license, having failed the written test the first time, I approached the counter only to meet with a very intense man. *Hmm*, I thought, *I need to pass this test, what can I do to humor him?* I noticed that not only did he have extremely close-set eyes, he also had exposed eyelids, which meant he didn't like his time to be wasted. He also had an oval forehead, often seen in gourmet cooks, and tight skin across the frame of his face, which indicated he liked things to be squeaky clean. So I asked him, "Do you enjoy cooking?"

"Why, yes," he said. "I do all the cooking at home. I'm a gourmet cook."

"Yes," I said, "and I expect you like things to be squeaky clean." A slight sparkle appeared in his eyes, and his mouth start to turn up into a smile. I had accomplished my goal!

We all meet people who have intense styles of communication, being under pressure adds to their intensity. Looking for facial clues will help you understand and relax them, thus producing positive results and better communication. When you walk away from your encounters with these individuals, you will be able to say to yourself, "Yes, my efforts worked." It will leave a smile on your face as well as on theirs.

Sometimes individuals with extremely close-set eyes focus on problems until they seem to become bigger than life itself. They create movies in their heads by replaying remarks or situations over and over again. If their feelings have been hurt, they dwell on this for hours, days, and even months. Add backward balance to this, meaning someone who has more head behind the ear compared with the amount in front of the ear, and now you have a person who will run the situation or the remark over and over in his or her mind until consumed by it. One person I encountered who has the above trait combination told me it took her down into a deep dark hole. This tendency would make her immensely depressed. Those of us who do not have these traits will see such people as unreasonable and get quite irritated by their behavior. Rather than do so, think of ways to relax that person and to get him or her to look at the bigger picture. Help the person focus on what to do next in order to move his or her life forward.

Low Tolerance individuals are quick to respond and at times very intense in their emotional involvement or responses. One often sees this trait in people who follow strong religious or spiritual causes or beliefs. Close and deep-set eyes can be seen in many followers of the Taliban and other deeply religious groups. Deep-set eyes indicate someone who takes life extremely seriously. People with these facial features become so focused on their beliefs or their causes that they fail to notice what else is going on around them; they lose perspective. When a number of people in the same group or meeting share this trait, they may have a tendency to fuel each other's passions, taking their intensity even deeper.

At times, Low Tolerance individuals will seem overly fussy about the smallest details. This becomes exaggerated if they have a pointed nose and tight skin over the frame of the forehead. Individuals with this trait combination will appear to be overly obsessive about neatness. As previously mentioned, a person with tight skin on the forehead tends to be a neat freak; a person with a pointed nose is extremely fussy. The movie star Meryl Streep has this trait combination. Several women I interviewed with these traits expressed their frustration when their husbands left "their stuff lying around." Whenever they tried to throw out things they considered "garbage," their husbands would retrieve these items from the trash. They resorted to putting the objects in empty cereal boxes to disguise them, and they even asked their neighbors if they could use their trash cans to throw their husbands' "stuff" away! These women were obsessive about clutter. When I asked what they would do if their husbands threw their own stuff out, the response was, "I'd kill him." When I asked them, "How do you think he feels about you throwing out his things?" they paused in surprise, never having considered their actions from that perspective.

Typically, people with fine hair (High Sensitive) and close-set eyes (Low Tolerance) become so focused on what is wrong or upsets them that they take things out of context. Their thoughts immediately go to what is wrong, and they'll worry about it over and over in their minds. If this is something to which you can relate, you might want to find an activity that takes you away from your concerns, such as practicing yoga, listening to your favorite music, or going for a walk, or a bike ride.

Let's not forget the positive side of the Low Tolerance trait. These close-set-eyed people make excellent teachers because they stay focused. They're not as scattered as their wide-set-eyed counterparts; they are great with detail. Wouldn't you want your dentist, editor, or accountant to have this trait? So if you're not good at detail yourself, look for someone with close-set eyes to handle the details for you. If they also are critical (outer corner of the eye lower than the inner corner), this will heighten their awareness of mistakes. When I first met my new dentist, I was relieved to see his eyes were close-set.

Melanie faced a challenging situation with a coworker that caused her a lot of stress at work and in her personal life. She attended one of my workshops. During the class we covered the Low Tolerance trait, to which she was able to relate. Afterward, she realized how her behavior was affecting her fellow coworkers. The next day at her job, rather than insisting things had to be done her way, she was more open to considering a different approach. It worked. She felt a huge load lift off her shoulders, and she got along much better with her coworkers. Her intolerance had been her biggest challenge. Her father was very rigid, and one of her fears was having a child with the same personality as her father. For the first time, she understood why her father was so challenging. She could now be more aware of her own traits and raise a child who would grow up without the rigid childhood she had experienced.

While appearing on a British television show, I remember speaking with a woman who suffered from sleep deprivation. Her eyes could not have been any closer together, plus she had an extremely narrow face. I explained to her why she became overly anxious and that many people with this same personality trait experienced the same level of anxiety. I then gave her some ideas about how to relax when she went to bed. She threw her arms around me and told me how much that little bit of information helped her. She felt understood.

Another woman I worked with had not driven her car for some time because she was paranoid about getting into the car and driving. This represents typical behavior for people who have extremely close-set eyes. She sent me her photo, and I noticed how close set her eyes were. I gave her some suggestions about how to cope with her fear of driving, one of which involved listening to a book on tape or to one of her favorite pieces of music to distract her while she drives. The next week, she overcame her fear and drove from London to Manchester (200 miles). She continues to drive today. What could have taken months or even years to resolve just took a photo and three e-mails.

It's not always possible to achieve such immediate results. However, simply explaining the traits gives my clients a better understanding and awareness of their overreactions and how to manage them. I always emphasize that other individuals who have this trait may experience the same level of anxiety. They don't feel so alone. Remember, choice always supersedes structure.

The Low Tolerance trait often is seen in careers such as dentistry. I remember speaking at an international dental conference and over two hundred pairs of beady eyes looked at me from the audience. It felt strange. Other careers where you might find many people with close-set eyes include accounting, teaching, psychology, photography, or any activity that requires detail and focus. You will find people who specialize in their line of work have extremely close-set eyes. Think about it; doesn't it make sense? This trait can also be seen in professional tennis, baseball, golf and volleyball players. Many of the people who compete in the Olympic Games have this trait. These individuals have a strong desire to win a medal, and they don't let anything distract them from that goal. They are extremely focused—and stay focused—on their goal for many years.

For example, we certainly saw John McEnroe's low tolerance on the courts when he was an active tennis player. Other tennis players, such as Andy Roddick, Andy Murray, Venus Williams, and many of the Russian tennis players, have close set eyes. It doesn't mean to say that wide-set-eyed people don't play as well; they just have to concentrate more on staying focused. Next time you watch a ball game, notice how many of the players have close-set versus wide-set eyes.

Famous Faces
Andy Roddick, John Kerry, Jennifer Aniston, Venus Williams

Relationships
If you have close-set eyes (Low Tolerance) and your partner has wide-set eyes (High Tolerance) try not to over react to situations. If your tolerant partner keeps forgetting to do something, ask him or her for a day or time for the project to be completed. If they

end up being late and keep you waiting, don't snap at them. You might say ahead of time that you'd really appreciate it if they would let you know if they are running late.

Children

If your child has Low Tolerance, provide time for him or her to break away from activities; the transition will help you meet with less resistance. Just taking this approach will avoid much of the conflict experienced when children are interrupted during activities without warning.

One little girl had traveled some distance with her parents for her appointment with me. When I explained to her parents about giving her "five-minute warning" prior to asking her to change from one activity to another, the child said, "Just my parents knowing that was worth the trip." This had definitely been a challenging issue between the parents and the child. They needed to give her time to "change gear."

If children have close-set eyes and a narrow face (builds confidence), they may become extremely anxious and hesitant in new situations. These feelings can escalate to the point of becoming fearful. Parents shouldn't brush off their child's concerns, therefore, by saying, "You'll be fine." Discover what is causing the anxiety. It may be something a friend said, or perhaps they are concerned they may not pass an exam or get the results you are expecting. The more you support your children, the better they will feel, and the more relaxed they will become.

While my close-set-eyed seven-year-old granddaughter was staying with us, we had a minor fire in the middle of the night. Knowing she had a tendency to become very anxious, I calmly explained what we needed to do and that all would be well. She immediately relaxed and stayed calm throughout the event. After the firemen left, she went back to bed and immediately fell asleep. When my son returned at four in the morning, he could tell there had been a fire and checked to see if all was well. To his surprise, everyone was fast asleep. If you stay calm, your child will too. If you have extreme anxiety, this could magnify the situation for your close-set eyed children.

Children with close-set eyes may enjoy hobbies such as needlework, quilting, model airplanes, photography, painting, or any detailed activity.

If you are a parent with the Low Tolerance trait, try not to over react to situations around your Low Tolerance child. This may cause them a lot of anxiety and the situation can get blown out of context.

Sales

Don't overwhelm your client with too many details at once. If you're running late for an appointment, make sure you call ahead of time. This will help to avoid them feeling annoyed. Not the way to start a meeting. Do all you can to be on time.

Careers

Careers that provide a good fit for this trait include teaching, dentistry, psychology, accounting, physician's assistant, medicine, or any job requiring the ability to work well with detail.

High Tolerance: Wide-Set Eyes

Individuals with wide-set eyes are extremely easy going and have a tendency to take on too many tasks at once. They come across as being relaxed and often put up with situations for too long. They overextend themselves, and consequently, they find themselves running late for appointments because they want to do "just one more thing" before they leave their homes or offices. Their friends and associates may see them as unreliable when in fact, they are really trying to fit in too many things at the last moment. Their challenge is to stay focused on the activity at hand and not get caught up in unrelated projects.

We often see this High Tolerance trait in political and business leaders and in people working in careers where they need to handle or oversee a number of ongoing projects. They have the ability to look at the big picture, and generally, they do not become overwhelmed by all the projects or interruptions that may come their way. They almost welcome them.

When I was at the doctor's office for a minor problem, I could not help but notice that the receptionist definitely was multitasking and handling this well. Not only did she have wide-set eyes, she had a ski jump nose, which indicates a person who loves to help people, and therefore, is good at customer-service-related jobs. Her profile fit her position well, and she was doing a great job. I am sure the patients appreciated her, since her attitude had a relaxing effect, and she was easy to get along with. Plus she had a good sense of humor to go with it all.

High Tolerance

If you have the High Tolerance trait, make sure you arrive on time for appointments. If you find yourself running late, call ahead of time to let the other person know. This avoids the irritation and cold looks that can meet you if you're late. Make sure you set boundaries and deadlines, and stick to them. Think first before committing yourself to yet another project.

Mary told me she found it difficult to concentrate and often became extremely scattered. She would start on one project, and then suddenly, she switches to something else. While making the bed, she would get distracted by her dog and take it for a walk, then come back and go on to something else without finishing making the bed. When working on a business-related project, she had a tendency to start off on one, and before she knew what had happened, she had moved on to the next or had gotten completely sidetracked. If you can relate and fall into this category, you likely have the

High Tolerance trait. To help you stay focused, create a list of the things you need to do, and stay with each task until it is completed.

Have you ever noticed that when you're just leaving on a trip with family or friends, often someone has just one more phone call to make? Or someone takes forever to get out of the door? That's the High Tolerance person. Needless to say, Low Tolerance individuals find their behavior really annoying. The person waiting in the car starts honking the horn to create a sense of urgency. This is not a good way to start out on a trip! Understanding and working with these traits can help, though.

Swing on Tolerance

When the corner of one eye is closer to the center of the nose than the other, this indicates a tendency to swing from Low to High Tolerance and vice versa. To determine if someone has a swing in tolerance, draw a line down the middle of the nose, then measure the distance between the eyes. First, measure the right side from inner corner to the center; second, do the same for the left side. Next, notice if one side measures greater than the other. If so, this indicates a swing in tolerance.

You'll find individuals with this mood swing mostly function on the tolerant side. However, when things get too much for them, they suddenly "snap." This change in personality seemingly comes out of the blue. Afterward, they feel guilty for losing their cool and are hard on themselves for being so intolerant.

If you have this trait and find yourself in this kind of situation, take some time out, focus on what needs to be done, and don't get caught up in the overwhelming situation. Typically, when a person experiences a swing in this trait, it also indicates that one parent was less tolerant than the other. Hence, the child inherits the differences.

If a coworker or family member suddenly snaps at you, immediately look at their eyes and see if there is a difference. They are probably in overwhelm suggest they take some time out. This will help them gather themselves together again.

Famous Faces
Edward Kennedy, Tony Blair, Oprah Winfrey, Hilary Clinton

Relationships
Tolerance plays an important part in how two people get along together. In a relationship, when two people exhibit similar levels of tolerance, the couple will have similar expectations. If, however, they have dissimilar tolerance traits, the Low Tolerance person will feel irritated by the laid-back, easygoing, High Tolerance attitude

of his or her partner. High Tolerance partners will see their Low Tolerance partners as overreacting, and after a while, they will become quite fed up with what they judged as extreme behavior. They may also feel their partners' "style" cramps their more laid-back style of living. This can cause a lot of issues in a relationship as well as creating intense home atmosphere—not good for either of them and certainly not good for any children in the household. It's not easy to turn off this type of overreaction, and I do not fault people who do tend to overreact. It's not their intent; it's a part of who they are—their makeup, if you will.

Some common relationship issues can arise when a High Tolerance person and Low Tolerance person enter into relationship. What was forgivable prior to moving in together, for instance, becomes irritating once they live together full time.

Solutions exist, though. If you are the High Tolerance partner in a relationship and find yourself running late, call ahead of time and let the your Low Tolerance partner know. If your partner asks you to do something, only agree if you really intend to follow through. Otherwise, the Low Tolerance person will nag at you for not doing so. If you are the High Tolerance one, try not to do things that will annoy your partner. If you are the Low Tolerance partner, then try to resolve the issues in a less irritated manner. Think about how it would feel if someone communicated to you in that manner. That's how your partner or children will feel. Find ways to resolve the situation, so that you get positive results. It will actually strengthen the relationship. Opposites can work in relationships if both are willing to work on their challenges.

Children: High Tolerance

Wide-set-eyed children are very easy going and quickly get distracted from what they are doing. This can become challenging at school as well as at home. They forget to do their homework, to feed the dog, and to tidy their rooms. If you send them on an errand that should only take a few minutes, they come back an hour later. Parents need to set deadlines for these children and make sure they keep them. Homework must be done first, before they go off and play with their friends. They can have no phone calls or visitors until chores are done.

When school-aged children have a combination of High Tolerance (wide-set eyes) and High Physical Motivation (long lower face) traits, plus short legs (very restless), they will exhibit a short attention span. Until both children and parents understand that this is a part of the child's genetic makeup, this trait cluster may be interpreted as a disruptive nature. Short-legged children have a hard time sitting down for long periods of time. They get very restless and need to get up and move around to balance their energy. Once they do so, these children are able to concentrate on their studies. If you are a teacher, suggest your students stand up and do some stretching exercises.

Mandy had this trait combination and found it difficult to concentrate in her early years at school. She constantly found herself in the principal's office and failing her schoolwork. At age thirteen, she began junior high school and started playing sports—a turning point in her life. From that moment, her problems stopped, and she began excelling in school. Sports had not been a part of her life prior to that time. If her parents had known earlier, they could have enrolled her in an after-school sports program.

So many schools in the United States are cutting back on their sports programs due to budgetary constraints. These programs provide an essential outlet for students' excess energy and restlessness. Given the opportunity to exercise, children will get better academic results, and they will be less disruptive both at school and home—no matter what their trait combination is.

This trait cluster and the lack of physical activity could explain some of the attention deficit disorder (ADD) problems we see in children today as well. For some children diagnosed with ADD, we may find that channeling their energy into sports or other such activities will make a significant difference to the quality of their lives.

Sales

When trying to sell something to a customer, it's helpful to look at their eyes and know how best to approach them based upon their tolerance level. High Tolerance customers will look at the big picture. If they have the analytical trait (covered eyelids), they will have lots of questions. They may have a tendency to arrive late for appointments, so you might want to call ahead and confirm the appointment, plus emphasize the need for them to be on time; whereas, when working with customers with close-set eyes (Low Tolerance), don't overwhelm them with too much detail.

The more you know how to best approach your client the greater the chances of increasing your sales. It will also help you build long lasting customer relationships.

Careers

People with this trait will be well suited for any career that involves multitasking. If you also have the Critical Trait (outer corner of the eye lower than inner corner), this indicates you would do well in careers where precision is needed as well, such as engineering, construction, electrolysis, editing.

Judgmental

Inner Corner of the Left Eye Higher Than the Right Eye
Unconventional

When the inner corners of both eyes are on the same level, this indicates a person has a fairly conventional nature. However, if the inner corner of one eye is set higher than the other, this indicates a person is unconventional. To accurately determine the trait, it has to be measured. These people don't follow the crowd and appear not to fit in. They have a less conventional approach to situations, and they do not like to do things the way others do them; they find doing so boring. The greater the differences between their two eyes, the more these individuals will want to travel the unconventional path. They often wonder why they are not more similar to their friends. Their challenge lies in learning to compromise when working with more conventional people.

This eye characteristic typically indicates the trait of a Judgmental person, someone with the tendency to pass judgment about something or someone, whether that determination is right or wrong. Note that while their words may sound like criticism, their judgments say more about how something should or should not be done than about the person they are judging. For instance, when Ron met a woman, he immediately made a judgment about details, like her hair being short or her earrings not working with her outfit. These judgments weren't about the woman's nature but about how she wore her hair and chose her accessories. This Unconventional or Judgmental trait bothered Ron all his life because he felt it wasn't good to judge everything. He found living with this trait challenging. He constantly judged people, and at times, this got in the way of making friends.

Ron had spent hours researching this issue on the Internet and speaking with psychologists to try and understand why he was so judgmental. Thus, he was rather surprised that within five minutes of meeting him, I already had recognized his judgmental nature. He looked at me in amazement and said, "Do you know how much I have researched that tendency, and you just took one look at me and saw that in me?"

The fact that I was able to identify this trait right away gave him some comfort that it wasn't something he had made up. As he suspected, it was a part of his genetic makeup.

We all pass judgement about people and situations to a certain degree; however, Unconventional individuals have a judgment about everything. This will include the quality of something or how something should or should not have been done. More conventional people, on the other hand, tend to be less judgmental and are more comfortable with a conventional approach.

The Judgmental person also has a creative nature. They are able to come up with new ideas or solutions to problems. We would expect to see this trait in people involved in artistic fields, such as film, writing, drawing, painting, and theater—any situation where creativity can be used.

Famous Face
Leonardo DiCaprio

Relationships
If an individual with the Unconventional trait has the High Risk-Taking trait (ring finger longer than index finger), and their partner does not meet their emotional needs, they may well seek affairs outside of their relationship. However, as one man shared with me, he knew this about himself, but it was more important for him to build a life-long trusting relationship with his wife. He made this his priority, and he never had an affair.

If you feel tempted to have an extramarital affair or to cheat on your partner, think of ways to redirect your drive. Take up a hobby that consumes your energy, such as sculpture, painting, woodworking, film, or photography. Try any activity that satisfies your unconventional approach to life. Or get involved with a sport, such as rock climbing, mountain biking, kayaking, sky diving, or some sort of fitness program.

Children
A fourteen-year-old girl with the Unconventional trait shared with me that she felt like a loner at school, and she has hardly any friends. She didn't "fit the mold." Fellow students didn't include her in their conversations or social activities. She spent much of her leisure time at home reading by herself. I suggested to her mother that she sign her up for classes where she would meet other students who have the same interests and abilities as herself, such as art and writing.

I have the Judgmental trait, and while at boarding school, my Unconventional nature made it hard for me to "fit in." Hence, my heart went out to her, and I understood how much she wanted to be with and accepted by her peers. Fortunately for me, I enjoyed sports; this became my social outlet in school. Why I didn't fit in became clear to me when I first had a personology profile assessment. Until then, I had always been puzzled about why I chose a different path. Now I understand, and like many others, I feel free to be who I am.

Children with this trait may make a name for themselves in history later if their unconventionality can be directed constructively. Parents must help them focus their Unconventional tendencies in a positive direction, so it becomes second nature for the children to do so later in life.

Sales
A client with the above trait may enjoy products or services that offer a unique approach or solution, such as one that would give them a niche market that sets them apart from other companies.

Careers
The Unconventional person is gifted in creative and artistic fields, such as art, film, graphics, design, writing, or any profession that does not require normal run-of-the-mill ideas. They may also tinker with new inventions. They enjoy careers that offer a unique approach.

Analytical

Eyelid Covered with Fold of Skin

Loves to analyze

Eyelid Completely Exposed

Likes to get to the point

A person's analytical nature can be determined by the degree to which the eyelids are visible—how much or how little of the eyelids you can see. Individuals who have eyelids completely covered by the fold of skin have extremely analytical natures, and they will want to know how and why everything works. In encounters with Analytical people, prepare yourself for lots of questions, and be able to back up your statements with facts.

Analytical

On the other hand, Low Analytical individuals, those with completely exposed eyelids, like Hilary Clinton, want you to get directly to the point or to the bottom line. If you talk on an on, they feel their time is being wasted. When you hear this in their voice and conversation, recognize they are ready to make the appointment, purchase the product, or do whatever is necessary to get things accomplished. Low Analytical people get extremely impatient with long-winded discussions or meetings. They like to get meetings over and done. If they run a meeting, expect it to be completed in half the time it would take if run by a High Analytical person.

High Analytical

High Analytical people need to look into all aspects of a situation or a new purchase before making a decision. They over analyze what they already know, and to others, this may seem a waste of time. They like to put other "spins" on what is said. This painstaking analytical procedure makes Low Analytical individuals impatient. They respond with, "Come on! Let's just get on with it." But High Analytical individuals can't do that.

High Analytical people love to take things apart and figure out how they work. They will not only study how a building or piece of equipment was constructed, they'll also go into every aspect of a project to understand why it was designed that particular way. When making a new purchase, they will research and compare quality, performance, and price.

Combine this trait with close-set eyes (Low Tolerance), a pointed nose (Fussy), and a down-turned nose (Skeptic), and this person will want to investigate everything until completely satisfied they have all the possible information.

When buying a car or a piece of equipment, the High Analytical customer will want to know down to the smallest detail how and why it functions. Be prepared for lots of questions. If they also have a pointed nose (Fussy), they will dig into everything until they are satisfied. Salespeople would do well to have printouts ready that cover all the possible questions and answers for prospective individuals with this trait to read. If you are presenting a new product or idea to a customer, and you notice they have this trait, you might want to begin your presentation by stating, "You look like a person who will have lots of questions." Present them with a product sheet first, and go through it with them. They will feel comfortable having the facts literally in hand, and they will be less likely to interrupt your presentation.

A woman who came to one of my workshops identified the Analytic trait in her boss. She dreaded meetings with him because she always felt he was interrogating her. Afterwards, she understood and no longer dreaded the meetings.

The High Analytical person enjoys games such as chess, bridge, and crossword puzzles. If the individual with this trait also has a pointed nose (Fussy), they tend to be extremely picky. This combination of traits, plus an oval forehead (good at maintaining projects), often is seen in people in health-related professions, such as nutritionists, dietitians, and chiropractors. Analytical Individuals who have pointed noses make good investigators or FBI agents. This trait combination offers a plus for any profession that includes investigation as part of the job profile. These people turn over every stone until they feel sure they have left nothing to dig up. Analytical people make great technicians and researchers, or they do well in any career that benefits from analytical probing.

Sometimes, a person with this analytical trait has a tendency to over analyze simple situations and make things more complicated. For example, something was wrong with my iron. You might think the first thing to check would be the plug. However, for my husband, who is an analytical person, this solution seemed too simple. He took the iron completely apart and carefully labeled each piece. He still could not uncover the problem, which prompted me to ask, "Did you check the plug?" Of course, he hadn't. I opened up the plug, and there lay the answer: The wires had separated.

If you are very analytical, when necessary, speed up the process. Understand that not everyone needs to know all the details to make a decision. Get to the point quickly. When on the phone, if a person appears to be cutting you off, this could signal that they want to get to the point. If you are in sales, listen for this clue with clients on the phone or in person, and remain aware of this trait.

I received a phone call from a man whom I thought was making general inquiries. After a few minutes he said, "Naomi, I just want to make an appointment."

Hmm, I thought, *This man must have exposed eyelids.* Sure enough, when I met him, I saw that my assessment had been accurate. I might have lost the sale had I continued talking to him and embarked on a lengthy explanation, rather than getting to the point and making an appointment.

If you are meeting with someone and have a number of questions, you might want to say, "I have a number of questions. Please, bear with me. It's important to go over them." This way, you make your needs known. If the other person is short on time, just go over the most important questions first, and set aside another time when you can go over the rest of them in detail.

Famous Faces
Richard Branson, Colin Powell, Margaret Thatcher, Martha Stewart

Relationships
Imagine being in relationship with someone so analytical that they have to know the reason for every little thing you do. If you are a Low Analytical partner, you will get fed up with all their questions. You'll roll your eyes as they continue to ask one question after another. If you are the High Analytical partner, get the hint. If the questions really aren't necessary, let them go or just say, "Bear with me for a while, I need to discuss the details."

You may just be sharing some news that you read in the local paper, but your High Analytical partner immediately wants to know the facts, where the information came from, and whether it came from a credible source—all that just because you wanted to share some local news. If you are analytical, that may sound reasonable. However, those with the opposite trait quickly become annoyed and respond, "Oh, forget it." As you can see, a High Analytical and a Low Analytical person in relationship can prove trying. If both partners are High Analytical they will enjoy each other's inquiring nature.

Children
Be patient with your children who have the High Analytical trait. They will have lots of questions. If you are Low Analytical (bottom line), be prepared to answer their questions, especially when it relates to homework.

Sales

If your client has the High Analytical trait, be prepared for a lot of questions. Try not to cut them off.

Careers

This would apply to all careers that would benefit from the need to analyze various aspects of the job. The High Analytical trait is often seen in the medical field, engineers, and researchers.

Low Analytical

When the eyelid is fully exposed, this indicates someone who wants to get to the bottom line. When they have enough information to go on, they become action driven. They like to get directly to the heart of the matter. If needed, they will go back and check the details later. Once they have grasped the concept, they prefer to act right away. They will ask why, but they will not necessarily take the time to deeply analyze the problem. They find long drawn-out explanations boring. They are more matter-of-fact and to the point.

Low Analytical

Sometimes, Low Analytical individuals may appear ruthless and cold because they like to get to the core of things quickly, ignoring the subtleties and the different facets others have meticulously researched for them. They like to cut through the red tape and get things accomplished. If you talk too long, they either will cut you off in the middle of a sentence or finish it for you. Others may find these actions rude, and they think that what they had to say was of little importance to the Low Analytical person.

People with this trait can also come across as rather aggressive, competitive, and in-your-face, particularly if they have a pointed nose (Fussy). They are more "in-your-face" people. Often, such people are trying to get others to see their point, but this can have the opposite effect when their posturing puts people off.

Ann's husband constantly interrupted her. She found this annoying, and she felt that what she had to say was unimportant to him. "Why do you keep interrupting me? I haven't finished yet. Why don't you want to hear what I have to say?" she asked him.

Her husband responded, "I already know what you're going to tell me. If you would only just get to the point!"

If you ever go into the hospital emergency room (hopefully as a visitor), notice that most of the doctors and nurses have exposed eyelids. They are good in crisis situations because they quickly evaluate what action to take and then say, "Come on, let's go." They like the excitement of what is going on around them, and enjoy the feeling of rising to the occasion. They like to cut through the red tape to get things done. In these situations, their actions are highly productive.

That said, nurses need to be careful about cutting off their patient in mid-sentence, or patients feel unheard. If a nurse asks how you are feeling, and you start to explain, but you get cut off in mid sentence, as a patient you will feel brushed off, unimportant, or not cared for. The nurse probably has heard the same response many times, knows the response as you begin to speak; hence, she cuts you off mid-sentence. If you recognize this tendency and are in the nursing profession, take the time and listen to your patients' questions or needs. This will help them feel more relaxed.

When Low Analytical Sandra runs a meeting, she immediately determines the issues, the problems, and what needs to be done next. She also decides how long the meeting should take, and immediately begins banging out the agenda. If others in the meeting want more discussion, she responds: "Why do we need to keep talking? Let's get to work." Sandra doesn't need all of the "story" before starting on the project. She quickly gets a sense of what needs to be handled. A lot is accomplished at her meetings, although some people probably leave feeling frustrated and still feeling the need for more discussion.

If you are more of a bottom line person, understand that others may need to know more information than you do before making a decision. Slow down your reaction time. Be prepared to explain in more detail for the analytical people. Particularly in a sales situation, this creates a feeling of trust. Just remember to be patient when others need more detail or discussion. Or you might say, "I know I move along quickly. You may have a lot of questions. Can we go over the most important ones first?" In this way you communicate your needs and acknowledge theirs.

While waiting for a shuttle bus one day, I noticed the young lady next to me had exposed eyelids and close-set eyes (Low Tolerance). *I bet she's studying psychology,* I thought. I asked her if she was in college and what was she studying.

"Oh," she said, "I'm studying psychology." I explained to her what I did and also mentioned that people with a vertical forehead (Sequential Thinker), like herself, often become gymnasts. She looked at me in surprise and said, "Yes, I was one of the top female gymnasts." Next time you watch a gymnastics competition, notice how many have exposed eyelids and vertical foreheads.

Many male physical therapists have exposed eyelids. Also many martial arts students have this trait.

Famous Faces
Anthony Hopkins, Andy Roddick, Nancy Pelosi, Condoleeza Rice

Relationships
Low Analytical partners may cut their High Analytical partners off in the middle of their sentence, which could really annoy them. Their partner may feel extremely hurt and may come to conclusions that what they have to say is unimportant to them. If both partners have this trait, then it won't present such an issue.

Children

You may find it annoying if your children constantly interrupt you. Keep in mind, they inherit the trait either from you or their other parent. Explain to them that they need to be patient and to listen to what other people tell them.

Sales

If you are a High Analytical person and your clients just want the bottom line, don't bog them down with lots of information. If you are more of a bottom-line person, learn to be patient with your more analytical clients. Don't cut them off, listen to their concerns. Make sure you answer any questions that come up.

Careers

People with this trait will enjoy and excel at any career that benefits from this extremely analytical tendency, such as jobs in research.

Critical Perception

High Critical Perception
Outer corner of eye lower than inner corner

Low Critical Perception
Outer corner of eye higher than inner corner

There lies a critic in all of us. However, critical behavior becomes extreme when the outer corner of the eye is lower than the inner corner. People with High Critical Perception tend to see every little error and wonder why others do not see these obvious mistakes. Nothing annoys them more than when other people are careless. Perfectionists by nature, these individuals not only expect perfection of themselves, but also of family members and coworkers. If the parents have the Critical trait, they can have quite an impact on their children, who can never seem to please such parents. Nothing is ever good enough.

On the other hand, if the outer corners of the eyes slant upward, individuals will notice achievements rather than mistakes. People with Low Critical Perception are far less critical.

Let's look at the affect that critical parents have on their children. No matter how hard he tried to get paternal approval, Michael's father, who had inherited the above trait, never gave his son any positive recognition. Michael could never live up to his father's expectations. His father constantly criticized him, saying he felt that he would never amount to much. When Michael spoke to his father about his constant criticism, he simply responded, "Your grandfather was a bastard, so I'm a bastard." He felt his father's treatment justified his own attitude toward his son.

Later, Michael decided to enroll in a life coaching course. This helped him immensely in coping with his father's negative attitude. The next time he met with his father, he refused to enter into the usual line of conversation; consequently, he had a more enjoyable visit. Even though his father still went through the same critical dialogue, Michael was able to step back and not engage in such a way that he fueled the fire or felt hurt or angry.

Sandra thought her High Critical mother did not love or want her because her mother verbally disapproved of her so much throughout her childhood. It wasn't until she was thirty years old that Sandra confronted her mother. Only then did she discover her mother loved her all that time. She regretted that it took her thirty years of her life to know her mother truly cared.

Ken, age forty, heard about my work and sent me his photo to be analyzed. I was immediately struck by his eyes—the outer corners of his eyes were lower than inner corner, which showed his Critical trait. Because this could be seen in both of his eyes, it suggested that he had two extremely critical parents. Indeed, he told me they had practically destroyed his spirit, and he currently was seeing a psychologist to help him get through the pain of those relationships. After looking at his photograph and noting the rounded outer edge of ear, which indicates a natural musical ability, I suggested he study music. As a child, his parents had believed that field held no future for him. Despite their opinions, he enrolled in the Los Angeles School of Music, only to receive more criticism from the instructors. When this proved too much for him, he dropped out of the program.

Highly Critical

After my assessment, which offered reassurance that he truly had a gift for music, Ken revived his interest in music. He now plays with a local musical group. A photo profile and my confirmation of what he already knew gave him the confidence to take up music again.

Although parents want the best for their children, they do not realize the impact their criticisms have on them. This was the case for a woman I met who also had the Critical trait in both eyes. She said her father was so critical of her on about everything she did that his reactions caused her to put her life on hold. She kept rerunning his constant criticizing in her head; she also had the Backward Balance trait (more head at the back of her ear compared with the front), which causes this type of mental "replay." At age seventy-two, she has decided to let go of her father's critical voice and do what she had always dreamed of doing—becoming an artist and coach. At long last, she began living her life. Parents mean well but they can have a profound effect on their child's life.

High Critical people affect their coworkers and employees as well as the other people whom they are in relationship with. For example, Bob, a perfectionist, owned a construction company. He really came down on his employees when they failed to notice mistakes in their work. He would rant, "You must be stupid not to notice such obvious mistakes. What's wrong with you?" This didn't exactly boost the morale of his workers. However, once he understood that he actually had the gift of seeing errors others didn't see, he backed off and only criticized workmanship if it was vital to the construction.

Bob also realized that his three failed marriages probably resulted from his constant criticism of his wives' efforts. They could never get things perfect enough for him, and his need to harp on little mistakes wore them down and damaged the relationship.

If you have inherited the Critical trait, find ways to look for the good in everyone and everything first—before you criticize. Realize that, at times, you can be your own worst critic. The words "never good enough," which often flash through your mind, don't support your own personal growth or that of your family members or coworkers. Praise others for what they have done, then make some helpful and supportive suggestions about what they might want to change next time. Think about what it feels like when someone criticizes you. If you're a parent, praise your child and acknowledge what they have done. If something is not quite right, you might say, "You've done a great job, there are a couple of things that you might want to change. May I make a suggestion?" Use these same strategies on yourself as well. Tell yourself often, "Job well done."

If you tend to be critical, use criticism for on-the-job situations, but learn to do so in a constructive way. Remember to give equal amounts of praise and acknowledge when a job is well done. Criticizing fellow workers too much or too often is counterproductive and results in hard feelings.

When the outer corner of the eye goes upward (Low Critical Perception), these individuals have a far less critical nature and often miss mistakes. This becomes even more noticeable if they also have wide-set eyes (High Tolerance). If you have this trait combination, get someone to double-check your work just to be on the safe side.

If you are a Low Critical person and tend to overlook mistakes, be more alert for possible flaws on the job. Double-check to make sure you have not overlooked an important fact before turning in work.

Famous Faces

Hugh Grant, talent show host Simon Cowell, Nancy Pelosi, Condoleezza Rice

Relationships

High Critical Perception constitutes one of the more challenging traits in relationships. More than a few couples have broken up when they found themselves ill-equipped for the challenge posed by this trait. When one partner constantly criticizes the other, at some point, the other person cannot take what feels like constant criticism anymore.

If you have this trait, become aware of how your criticism affects the person with whom you live. Learn to analyze the importance of what you criticize. If you are criticizing something unimportant, let it go.

Often, we put on our best manners, or show our best faces, at work or with friends. We let our hair down when we get home; thus, our families or partner take the brunt of our day's experiences. If we have the High Critical trait, this means we save all that critical energy for use on those we love most. That's a sure-fire recipe for relationship disaster. If you have this trait, it's up to you to turn it off when needed. If your partner has this trait and you find yourself being criticized, try not to take it too personally. This may not be their intent. Underneath all this, they may have a big heart and sincerely care about you.

Children

If you are High Critical parent, be aware of the impact your criticism has on your children. If your children have inherited the critical trait, teach them how to use it constructively; emphasize the gift (the ability to find errors and flaws), not the challenge. As one person put it, she learned how to turn off the trait when not needed, although this is often easier said than done.

Teachers with this trait must be sensitive when criticizing students' work; the criticism can prove devastating. Make sure you praise your student first; then point out what they need to change.

I met a seventy-five-year-old woman and immediately noticed in her face an appreciation of drama (eyebrows flared upward). I asked her if she had worked in the theater. As it turned out, at age thirteen, she had received an award for "best actress" in a school play. She was thrilled and dreamed of performing on stage as an adult. Her teacher at the time told her, "Don't let that award go to your head. You're not that good an actress." Her dream was crushed by her teacher's words, and her parents did not support her acting either. She never pursued a career in theater, but I told her it was not too late to live out her dream.

Sales

If you have the High Critical Perception trait and work as a real estate agent, and you are aware that a property has a number of things that need to be fixed, point this out to your client ahead of time. This will help you move them through the process and not fixate on the "mistakes" inherent in the house as you show it—a focus that won't help you render a sale. However, this focus might help a client wanting to sell, rather than buy.

If you find yourself working with a client who quickly points out mistakes in your document, don't take it personally. Simply fix the issues as soon as you can. Keep in mind, mistakes jump off the page at them. Make sure you thank your client if they bring something to your attention that needs to be corrected.

Careers

Looking at this facial characteristic in a positive light, the Critical Perception trait is a gift. Individuals with this trait make great editors, cameramen, engineers, construction supervisors, and surgeons. This includes any profession requiring precision. Wouldn't you want these people as your airplane or car mechanic? Wouldn't you want your surgeon to have this trait? High Critical people make good literary, film, music, and art critics because their analytical capability adds insight and perspective to their work. I gave a talk at an electrolysis conference; nearly every one of the attendees had this trait.

Serious

Serious-minded
Deep-set eyes

Less Serious
Eyes set forward

Individuals who have deep-set eyes take life, work, and responsibilities extremely seriously. They become quickly annoyed when other people appear more flippant about situations. They reason, "If I don't take things on, who will?" They feel this is their destiny. Add close-set eyes (Low Tolerance) to this facial feature, and at times, they feel responsible for carrying the world on their shoulders.

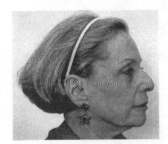

Serious

Individuals with the High Serious-Minded trait are more thoughtful and reflective, particularly if they also have close-set eyes (Low Tolerance) and fine hair (Sensitive). With this trait cluster, small issues become more significant and completely absorb them. They do not always see the humorous side of life and need to learn how to lighten up and to have fun. If you are a High Serious-Minded individual, take up a hobby or physical activity to help yourself relax and have fun.

Individuals on the opposite pole of this trait take situations less seriously and are more light-hearted. Serious individuals may see others as making light about situations, which in their views, need to be taken seriously.

Joanne had a tendency to take on everybody's problems. She wanted to feel needed, and she became quite depressed if she could not express this need in some manner. Her serious nature left her feeling drained and heavy. I encouraged her to imagine stepping into an area of her life where everything felt lighter and to describe that feeling. After a moment, she responded that it felt good. "It feels like another person inside of me that wants to get out. It's like being a kid again," she said.

If you are a Serious-Minded individual, remind yourself to find ways that will help you look at the lighter side of life. Also, share the responsibility of your problems with others.

Famous People
John Kerry, Abraham Lincoln, Cher

Relationships
In relationships, Low Serious-Minded individuals may feel weighed down by their serious partners. They may find the level of seriousness so heavy to the point where it stifles the relationship. The Serious person will see the less-serious partner as being too flippant during what they feel is a serious discussion.

Children
The Serious-Minded trait may not become evident until a child becomes a teenager. Combine this trait with close-set eyes (Low Tolerance) and a narrow face (Builds Confidence), and children with these facial features can turn into great worriers. Both parents and teachers need to reassure such children or teenagers that all is well and help them learn not to take on other people's responsibilities.

Sales
If you are working with a very serious client, avoid making frivolous remarks about concerns they share with you. It could annoy them.

Careers
No specific careers require this trait.

Emotional Expression

High Emotional Expression
Large irises

Low Emotional Expression
Small irises

Most of us look at a person's eyes first when we meet them. The eyes send many messages. Are they open and honest, or beady and suspicious? Do they dart about or focus upon the person to whom they are speaking?

People with sparkling eyes are more approachable; they simply seem friendlier. Individuals with cold piercing eyes appear to look right through us. The eyes send signals we unconsciously read and from which we make judgments based on past experiences.

Children usually have irresistible large irises. This gives their faces a wonderful look of innocence. We all want to reach out and touch them just to be close to the love and affection that pours from their eyes. Such large irises tend to feel open and loving, and at an early age, children express a lot of emotion. If they are exposed to physical or emotional abuse or under any prolonged stress, the irises become smaller in size. You see this in children raised in countries experiencing a lot of unrest or physical and emotional abuse.

One woman I met had cold piercing eyes. She felt misunderstood by people and wondered why. In fact, it took a while for people she met to move beyond what appeared to them as her cold demeanor. Yet underneath her eyes lies a warm and caring person. If you find yourself reacting or turning away from certain people, look at their eyes—actually, look beyond their eyes, which may belie their actual personality. Give them a chance. Get to know them first, then decide about their personality.

Emotional Expression

The amount of emotion a person expresses is determined by the size of the iris, the colored part of the eye, in relationship to the sclera, the white part of the eye. The larger the iris, the more likely an individual will show and express what they feel. People with large irises tend to be extremely emotional; and generally, they are more open to sharing their feelings, whether that means showing sorrow, happiness, or enthusiasm. Affectionate by nature, they are demonstrative as well.

At times, though, High Emotional Expression individuals become overly emotional, especially when this trait is combined with Low Tolerance (close-set eyes) and Dramatic (eyebrows flair up on the outer edge) tendencies. These individuals will "fall in love" within the first few minutes—maybe even seconds. They also get caught up in other people's emotional situations to the point that they become emotionally drained and exhausted. When emotions run high, these individuals can blow a situation completely out of context or proportion, and this tendency can be exaggerated if the above trait is combined with the Low Tolerance trait (close-set eyes).

High Emotional
Expression

High Emotional Expression people have this trait in a variety of ways. John described his wife, who had this trait, as requiring "high emotional maintenance." She needed reassurance several times a day that he loved her. This emotional need stemmed not from a sense of insecurity, but rather, from her emotional personality. If John did not express his affection for her, she thought she had done something wrong, or worse, that he didn't love her anymore. She might even get upset enough to think, heaven forbid, maybe he was having an affair!

When Susan, a High Emotional Expression individual, felt pleased with projects she completed at work, she related the experience to the times when "I had to show mom I had cleaned my room." She sought out her supervisor to show him what she had accomplished because she needed his approval. If he didn't acknowledge her efforts, she felt extremely let down. As a child, she often had the sense that her emotions were not reciprocated.

Susan lived in a city for a while, but it drove her crazy. Seeing so many homeless people raised within her a sense of needing to help save the world, but she knew she couldn't accomplish this feat. The stress of this internal conflict proved too much for her to bear on a daily basis. She felt so overwhelmed that she remained inside, rather than being reminded of the suffering in the city. If, like Susan, you tend to get overly emotional about other people's problems or situations, step back and try not to get so involved.

Children generally are born with large irises. However, those who live in war zones, such as in Afghanistan, Palestine, Iraq, and other areas of extreme unrest, have the whites of their eyes exposed under the irises. This indicates the child (or adult) is under a lot of stress. If the white shows under only one iris, this indicates the first stage of stress. If you can see it under both, this shows long-term stress. Such individuals may feel melancholic.

Unlike people with large irises, people with small irises do not let their emotions sway their decision-making process. These Low Emotional Expressive individuals deal more dispassionately with others. They make decisions with their heads rather than their hearts. Their eyes are less expressive, and they run the risk of appearing indifferent, cold, or unemotional. These people keep their feelings hidden under the surface. They are not as outwardly affectionate, and they find it difficult to express what they feel. They stay outwardly calm and work well in emotional situations. They pride themselves on their own emotional control.

Often times, this trait may indicate verbal or physical abuse in a person's past. When this happens, over time, the iris becomes smaller. It can take years before it returns to its original size after such trauma. A young lady at one of my workshops had this trait. She was amazed when I mentioned that I thought she had gone through some extreme abuse. Only her close friends and family knew about what had happened to her.

Famous Faces: High Emotions
Jennifer Aniston, Richard Gere, Julia Roberts

Relationships
Low Emotional Expression individuals must learn to share their feelings with their partners. You cannot expect them to second-guess what you are thinking and feeling. It may feel difficult at first to do so, so take one small step at a time. Individuals with this trait may feel psychologically naked when forced to express their emotions. To them, expressing their feelings seems like revealing everything about themselves for the world to see. It might be hard for them to break down the protective barrier they have built around themselves and their feelings.

For these reasons, it takes a while to get to know Low Emotional Expression individuals. Over the years, they have learned that people just don't seem to care about their feelings. So rather than risk rejection, they keep their emotions to themselves. In personal relationships, this can be somewhat challenging. Everyone else could be breaking down emotionally around them, and they will pride themselves on not showing how they feel, Whereas, the High Emotional Expression partner may feel they are not getting the reassurance that their Low Emotional partner cares about them. They feel an indifference or coldness. If this individual has thin lips, this will add to their not expressing what is going on inside. They "button up" and keep it to themselves.

Children

Children can get overly emotional about situations that are going on with friends at school or a remark that may have been made to or about them. If they have close-set eyes, the remark could really impact them. Find ways to help them let the incident go.

Sales

If your client has this trait, you might want to use words or phrases that will stir the emotional side of them. This could influence the decision to purchase the project or service from you.

Careers

The High Emotional Expression trait would be an asset in any career that necessitates working with people. Your client will feel comfortable in your presence, especially if you have Magnetic Eyes (eyes that sparkle).

Magnetism

High Magnetism   Low Magnetism
Eyes sparkle   No sparkle in the eye

The deeper a person's eye color, and the more sparkle in that eye, the more magnetic a person's personality. However, don't confuse the Magnetic trait with the Emotional Expressive trait that is related to the size of the iris. Magnetism is related to the eye color and the amount of warmth and sparkle that can be seen in the eye.

Just as with the Emotional Expressive trait, when we meet people who have sparkling eyes, we immediately feel attracted to them. Strangers will pour out their life stories to these individuals. Men and women who have these magnetic eyes are thought to be flirtatious. One woman I interviewed said she found it annoying when men came up and flirted with her; she thought they had ulterior motives and didn't want to get to know her. In her early twenties, she tried to look as unattractive as possible to turn men off.

Many a couple has told me this flirtatious quality posed a huge issue in their marriage. For instance, Tom was convinced his wife Carole deliberately flirted with other men at parties or social gathering. This issue escalated to the point where Carole no longer wanted to attend parties because doing so always created conflict between her and Tom. Plus Carole felt strange when she went out socially; men constantly approached her, believing she was flirting with them; while women avoided her, feeling threatened by her seemingly flirtatious behavior.

Add low-set eyebrows to this trait (Affable), and it adds to the magnetism. A magazine editor in England asked me take a look at a photo of a woman who captured everyone's attention in the audience during her performance at a talent show. She had the magnetic eyes, low-set eyebrows, as well as several other facial features that would make her quite appealing to audiences.

If you have deeply colored eyes that twinkle and sparkle, use body language to avoid unwanted attention. Make it clear as soon as someone advances toward you that you are not available—unless you are! Take a couple of steps back, physically distancing yourself from the person. Fold your arms across your chest, or use a firm voice.

If you are in relationship and your partner gets jealous due to the attention your Magnetic trait naturally attracts, ask him or her how they would feel if you exhibited the same level of jealousy toward them. Find a solution you both can work with before the situation gets out of hand. Many movie stars have this magnetic quality which I am sure creates issues in their relationships. Notice how many of the men have sparkling eyes and low-set eyebrows. This adds to their appeal as an actor, especially in romantic roles.

I met a woman at a workshop who had extremely cold-looking eyes, the opposite of the Magnetic trait. She was surprised that I approached her because people did not usually do so. She told me she often felt misunderstood and isolated in social gatherings. If you have cold-looking eyes, wear flattering colors or seek out a color or image consultant. When you wear the right colors, it helps soften the austere message you radiate and makes you look more approachable.

High Magnetism

Famous Faces
Sarah Palin, Julia Roberts, Mel Gibson

Relationships
If your partner has the Magnetic trait, don't presume he or she is flirting with other people. These individuals naturally draw people to them because they look friendly.

Children
When children have High Magnetism trait, they quickly learn how to take advantage of this asset by appealing to the parent most susceptible to their charms. Despite your children's adorable faces, parents need to make sure they stay within the boundaries they have set for them. Children constantly test those boundaries to see how much they can get away with.

Sales
In sales situations, magnetic eyes stir up the emotions, especially if the salesperson also has low-set eyebrows (Affable). These features, along with the competitive trait, provide great assets in sales. If your client has the High Magnetism facial feature, notice the amount of expression in their eyes. This will tell you how the sale or presentation is progressing.

If your client has the Low Magnetism trait, don't let the perceived coldness create distance in communication. They may be very friendly.

Careers

High Magnetism offers an advantage for people who work in sales and marketing also customer service. They can be very persuasive, especially in face-to-face negotiations. This trait also provides an advantage in counseling and the ministry, as well as in many theatrical roles, such as romantic parts, and for workshop leaders. Magnetism offers a great asset for anyone working with people, such as acting, teaching, or coaching.

Chapter Five

The Nose

The Ministrative Nose

Ski Jump Nose
Enjoys helping others

Noses come in all shapes and sizes—some small and cute, others large and distinguished (although some owners of large noses may not see it that way). Some people sport pointed noses, like Meryl Streep, while others have more bulbous ones, like Bill Clinton, William Hague, and Oprah Winfrey. In some cultures, noses of a particular shape, such as the Roman (convex) nose, are more dominant. However, you can still find people with Roman noses in all nations, including Scotland, India, Poland, and Arab countries.

As with other facial features, the nose tells us something about a person's personality. Cosmetic surgery on the nose, however, does not change an individual's personality. If a Roman-nosed individual has the bridge of his or her nose straightened, he or she will still want to be the boss and will be on the lookout for a bargain, since these traits commonly accompany this facial feature.

The ski jump, or Ministrative, nose indicates individuals who naturally enjoy helping others. You will see them working as nurses, sales representatives, waiters or waitresses, receptionists, customer service representatives, and volunteers. Individuals with this trait, automatically respond to other people's needs and requests. They are the first to raise their hands when requests go out for volunteers. They enjoy helping the sick and have an instinctive feel for nursing, especially when the Ministrative trait is combined with High Conservation (oval forehead). If someone needs help, they immediately drop what they are doing and are "right there." Human values come first to them; they put other's needs before their own, and sometimes, even before their family's needs. They need to learn to say "no" and let others volunteer.

Ministrative individuals have a hard time charging for their services. Not good at money management—from a use or value perspective, those in business for themselves who have this trait will find their greatest challenge in asking clients for money. This applies to both men and women. Ministrative individuals are more than likely to say, "Have it for free, or pay me next time." They like to avoid the subject of money. Balancing the checkbook is certainly not high on their list of priorities.

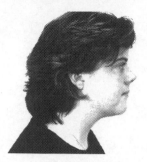

Ministrative Nose

If in business for themselves, Ministrative individuals might want to consider having a partner or hiring an accountant to handle the finances. I have met a number of men and woman who decided to go into business for themselves, and they struggled to make their businesses work not because they didn't have a good idea or an appealing product, they simply did not handle money well. They felt uncomfortable charging what everyone else was charging.

The unwillingness not only to handle money, but also to spend it wisely, posed a huge issue for one couple. The husband with the ski jump nose was such a spontaneous spender, an aspect of not managing money wisely, that his wife had to set up a separate bank account where he could not access their money. She decided to give him an allowance. She took these measures, so he wouldn't spend until they had nothing left in the bank. Ten years later, they still have this arrangement.

If Ministrative people also have Low Acquisitiveness (ears flat against the head) and a Generous nature (large lower lip), they may give away their last penny. They feel what they do deserves no financial reward. They focus only on the human value of their actions.

Ardelesa, a Ministrative person who owns an accounting business, had a really hard time collecting on the money owed for her services. In several cases, her accounts receivable were outstanding for over a year. She knew her clients were short of cash and did not want to press them for payment.

Another person I interviewed said she felt guilty about charging people. Clearly a Ministrative person, she thought if her rates were too expensive, her clients would not come back.

"What can I do to help?" is Anne's usual mantra. She has a hard time accepting that folks manage quite well without her. She has excellent skills for facilitating events, and enjoys this activity, but she feels uncomfortable having people report to her. Delegating tasks to others represents a challenge for her.

Ministrative individuals volunteer their services for nearly every cause that comes along, then find themselves overextended and wonder why. At times, helping other people simply means that such people never get anything done for themselves. Their challenge revolves around delegating tasks to others. A vice president of a steel company who had this trait said managing people posed one of his biggest job challenges. It didn't come naturally to him. He found it uncomfortable being in a management position, yet he had no option other than to assume it, unless he wanted to leave the company. The company was owned by his brother who was more Administrative (Convex Nose).

Other people take advantage of this behavior; the Ministrative person becomes their "go-fer." I visited this corporate vice president's steel company, and I watched as he constantly waited hand and foot on the other departmental vice presidents. He also was the first person to help me load up my car.

While visiting Boston, my husband and I got lost. It wasn't long before a woman came up to offer her assistance. She took at least twenty minutes of her time to tell us what sights to visit, how to find them, and to offer us additional information about the city. As you may have guessed, she definitely had a ski jump nose. One doesn't need to have a ski jump nose to help others, but those with this facial feature do so as a natural and spontaneous gesture.

If you have the Ministrative trait, keep in mind that you don't have to volunteer or contribute to every cause. Learn to "stop doing" for every needy person. Make sure you charge the full market price for your services; don't give your time away or under price yourself. If you charge the full price, people will place more value on what you have to offer. Set priorities and delegate tasks to other people; you don't have to take it all on yourself. If balancing your checkbook poses a problem for you, either hire a bookkeeper or sign up for a class on money management. This last suggestion is particularly valuable if you have the trait combination of Low Acquisitiveness (ears flat against your head) and being a Generous (full lower lip) individual.

Famous Faces
Condoleezza Rice, Bob Hope, singer Geri Halliwell

Relationships
The opposites of this trait in relationships can create issues. The Administrative (Convex Nose) person, will see their Ministrative partner as wasting money on what they deem as unnecessary purchases, or the partner with the Administrative trait and thin lips (Concise) will be very tight with money almost to the point of being stingy. This could also pose a relationship issue.

Children

Children are usually born with a ski-jump shaped nose. If their parents have more convex noses, the chances are the child's nose will be that shape by the time they are fully developed.

Sales

When selling a product or service to a person with a ski jump—shaped nose, emphasize how the product or service will help the customer.

Careers

Ministrative people tend to be good at nursing, administration, volunteering, waiting tables, customer service, social services, hosting, and working with children. They also enjoy volunteering for a cause. If they are in a management position, they will be more supportive of their team. As managers, they need to learn how to delegate tasks to their fellow workers.

The Administrative Nose

Convex Nose
Likes to be in charge

The Administrative trait, or someone with a Roman or convex nose, wants to be the boss. When this trait is really pronounced, Administrative individuals also will put price tags on everything. How much does it cost? Is worth it? Where can I get it for less? Finding a bargain makes their day. They are highly concerned with material values, and they try to think of ways to manipulate this to their advantage. To some people, they will appear impersonal and materialistic.

Administrative individuals work well in finance and business and best where organizing is needed and value for money comes first. They do well at delegating tasks to others and enjoy overseeing projects. These individuals fare well in careers such as accounting, appraising, and management. They can serve, but they find it confining to have careers in just a service position. Administrative personalities are not generally waiters or receptionists. If you hire individuals with this trait for a predominantly service position, they may not last long, or they may end up running the show.

I heard a group of women complaining about a new hire. "She's already trying to run the department," they said. This fact was causing bad feelings among the longer-term employees. The new employee didn't seem a good fit and had been hired for the wrong position—one that was not management related. If this had not been the case, this person would have been aware of how her fellow employees were reacting to her slightly bossy nature or would not have been trying to "manage."

I was browsing through the market at Covent Garden in England and noticed that nearly all of the stall owners had convex noses. In many small convenience stores, you will notice the shop owners have this feature as well. During an event in San Francisco, I happened to peek in at a pawn brokers' conference. I noticed the

Administrative Nose

majority of the attendees also had this facial feature. Next time you pass a pawn broker shop, pop in and check the owner's nose!

Some say a person can have a "nose for money." Now you know what to look for. That said, this doesn't mean that a person with a concave nose cannot be successful in business, neither does it mean that a person with a convex-shaped nose is guaranteed business success. Ministrative individuals will need to make sure they charge the going rate and meet their own financial goals. They can succeed; it just takes more determination. Administrative individuals can fail at business just as easily as anyone else. If they have the High Risk-Taking trait (ring finger longer than index finger), they may risk everything to the point that they lose their business.

If Administrative individuals also sport thin upper and lower lips (Low Automatic Giving) they come across as being tight with their money. They won't spend a penny more than necessary, and they won't like to buy for the sake of buying. To others, they appear stingy. One man I met with this trait combination thought presents were unnecessary; he did not like giving gifts for the sake of gift giving. However, he was quite prepared to spend a lot of money on his favorite hobby.

Janice said her husband had these traits, and she found him extremely stingy. Prior to speaking to me, she thought the stinginess came from his family upbringing. While on a trip together, her husband bought two T-shirts—one for himself and one for her. Afterwards, he asked her to pay him back for her T-shirt. This took her by surprise, since she thought hers had been a gift. (Yes. He was serious about her paying him back.)

Another time, a couple came in to have a relationship profile completed, and I noticed that the husband had the Administrative nose and very thin lips. I knew he was tight with money. I suggested he surprise his wife with a bunch of flowers or a bottle of wine. Her eyes lit up with expectation. About a week later, I receive a phone call from his very excited wife who said that she had received a bunch of flowers from her husband—on the computer! Eventually, he did give her a real bunch of roses, but it felt difficult for him to do so.

I observed this trait combination in one of my students. Later, when we discussed this, he confessed that he found it extremely difficult to give. In his mind, giving represented too frivolous an activity. At the end of my workshop, he gave each of us a box of chocolates and said, "I really am trying to be more generous." His gift was greatly appreciated by everyone.

If you have the Administrative feature or trait, try not to put a price tag on everything, especially within your family. Consider doing some volunteer work, and enjoy the reward of helping others in need. If you tend to be tight with your money, surprise your partner or friend with a bunch of flowers, bottle of wine, or an appropriate gift. Think of other ways you could contribute. Refrain from putting money and business first. Watch your tendency to be stingy, especially with family and friends.

When the Administrative trait is combined with a wide face (High Self-Confidence) and high-set eyebrows (High Selective), such people may appear intimidating. You will seldom see this person in the nursing profession, unless they are the head nurse. I find many of the Olympic athletes have this trait. They certainly have to raise large sums of money to support their desire to compete in the games. For example, the swimmer Michael Phelps has this shaped nose.

If this trait is combined with the High Competitive (wider head at the back than the front) trait, these individuals make good fund-raisers.

Famous Faces
John Kerry, Henry Kissinger, Barbara Streisand, author J. K. Rowling

Relationships
If the two people in a relationship have the opposites of this trait, it may well cause problems. One will want to spend all the money now while they can still enjoy it, and the other person will want to hold on to their money. One will balance the checkbook, while the other person won't know how much is in the account.

Children
This trait is not developed in children until they are teenagers. However, they may well exhibit a bossy nature, especially to their siblings. This could cause some disagreements between their brothers or sisters. You might suggest that they not be quite as bossy so that it will avoid any conflict.

Sales
If you notice that your client has a convex-shaped nose, emphasize the value of the product or service you are selling will bring to your client. You might also add something extra or offer a discount to close the deal.

Careers

People who have an Administrative trait plus the conservation trait (oval forehead) make good project managers. They also enjoy investing, fund-raising, or business administration. The latter includes any career that involves management and investments. People with this trait cluster make good lawyers, business developers, CEOs, and CFOs of companies. If they have the Low Tolerance (close-set eyes) trait as well, they may enjoy accounting.

Administrative/Ministrative Nose

Straight Bridge

When an individual has a straight bridge, this will indicate a combination of both the Administrative and Ministrative traits. This facial feature is often seen in stockbrokers, bankers, middle managers, and teachers. When combined with the Pioneering (straight outer edge of ear) trait, these individuals enjoy business consulting or owning their own business. Their personality includes a blend of both the desire to serve and the ability to administrate over projects, but not to the same degree as someone who scores high on either trait.

Administrative/
Ministrative

Famous People
Barack Obama, Gordon Brown, television newscaster Katie Couric

Relationships
This trait offers a good balance in relationships. This person will not feel the need to always be in charge of situations.

Children
This trait is not fully developed until they are in their teens.

Sales

If your client has this trait, emphasize the value of the service or the product you offer, and include how it will help them in their business.

Careers

This trait is seen in all careers.

The Nose for News

Bulbous Nose
Inquisitive

When we think about characters like Santa Claus (known as Father Christmas in England), Gnomes, and Mickey Mouse, they all have extremely rounded noses. Have you ever seen any of these characters with a sharp pointed nose? Probably not because a sharp nose indicates a very different kind of character.

The Nose for News

The more round or bulbous the nose, the nosier the person. Individuals who have this facial feature are simply inquisitive and love to discover the latest information. Other people see them as extremely nosy or as people who can't keep their noses out of other people's business.

You may notice when you are reading something, your bulbous-nosed friend often peeks over your shoulder to see what you're reading. Some find this annoying; however, these people are merely being curious.

Next time someone leans over your shoulder to see what you are doing, before you react, check out their nose. Then quietly say to yourself, *Oh, it's their nose. They can't help but be curious. It's their nature.*

Famous Faces
TV host Jon Gosselin, Jimmy Carter, actress Martine McCutcheon

Relationships
The Inquisitive person may nose into their partner's activities. They want to know about everything their partner is doing, which could be interpreted as being too nosy.

Children

The Inquisitive trait develops once children reach their teens. Their friends may interpret their natural curiosity as them wanting to know all about their private lives, especially if their parents also have the Inquisitive trait.

Sales

If you have an overly curious customer, with many questions, who appears nosey at times, and they have this trait, just be patient with them.

Careers

People with this trait do well in any career that would benefit from their inquisitive nature, such as real estate, nursing, investigation, coaching, or counseling.

The Fussy Nose

Very Fussy
Likes things to be very clean and neat

The Fussy trait is indicated by a pointed nose. The more pointed the nose, the fussier the individual. If this trait is combined with skin stretched tightly across the forehead and frame of the face, like Dick Cheney, these individuals will come across as being overly fussy. This picky behavior trait is heightened if the person also has the Low Tolerance (close-set eyes) and the High Critical (outer corner of the eye lower than the inner corner) traits.

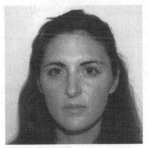

Fussy Nose

Jennifer acknowledged that she was extremely picky—towels had to be folded just right, books had to be angled perfectly and she couldn't stand clutter. Yesterday's newspapers left lying on the floor drove her crazy. Anything that was not being used had to be thrown away. When she put clothing out for the Salvation Army to pick up, she made sure they were folded immaculately. This gracious touch showed respect for the Salvation Army and the next user, but it also demonstrated her need to be clean and tidy.

When individuals become obsessive, they need to be aware of their own behavior and be open to doing something about it. Negative comments from others or pointing a finger at the Fussy person aggravates the situation, and it doesn't help the Very Fussy person behave differently. These individuals also tend to over react to situations. If you have this trait, try to realize that not everything has to be perfect.

If you have the above trait cluster, remember that not everyone has the same expectations. When you don't need such high standards (which may be most of the time), relax and enjoy what is going on around you.

Famous Faces

Dick Cheney, Martha Stewart, J. K. Rowling, Meryl Streep

Relationships

If you have this trait, keep in mind that not everyone has the same need to be so "squeaky clean." This can pose a challenge in relationships, particularly if one person is messy and the other has the Very Fussy trait. The Fussy person will constantly nag their partner to pick up, and this can become difficult for both partners to handle without getting annoyed with each other.

Children

If one child has this trait and other children in the family do not, the less fussy siblings will find their brother or sister extremely annoying. This could easily lead to arguments and accusations. Parents need to point out to the Fussy child how aggravating their behavior can seem to others.

Sales

A client with the Very Fussy trait could be extremely picky, so be patient and direct their attention to what works.

Careers

Fussy people excel at careers with the FBI, as dietitians and pharmacists, and in the fields of medical science research.

The Skeptic

Down-turned Nose
Questions everything

Straight Nose
Not as skeptical

When a person's nose turns downward, like those of Meryl Streep, Madeleine Albright, and Steven Spielberg, it indicates a Skeptical individual who tends to question everything. Such people do not accept things at face value. They need proof first. To others, they may appear to be distrustful.

If you are presenting Skeptical individuals with a new concept or idea, make sure you completely satisfy their questions and present them with all the facts first. Once you have done so, you can quickly win them over. Skeptical individuals are often amazed at the trusting nature of some people; they think it is only natural to question things thoroughly before making a commitment.

Skeptical individuals have a tendency to pour cold water on ideas, a behavior that can crush the enthusiasm of others. That is not their intent, however; it is frequently the effect they have on more-trusting people.

This trait can seem challenging in relationships. Skeptical individuals need to learn how to listen and support someone who shares ideas with them. After they have done so, they can offer creative suggestions and cautions. They must do this, however, before taking action or a stand on the situation. Others may perceive their skepticism as criticism, and this can bring out defensive behavior in their partners, for example.

If you are more skeptical, make sure your comments do not come across as being non-supportive to someone else's new idea. Get the whole story and all the facts before judging or making up your mind. Try listening to what the other person has to say first, and then ask them if they would like to hear your opinion. This will avoid misunderstandings or an emotional response like, "Oh,

The Skeptic

you never think my ideas are any good." Remember to keep an open mind and then offer a comment if needed.

When you deal with Skeptical people, remember, they have the need for proof or substantiation. If you present them with a new idea or concept, make sure you provide all the important facts. To them, it seems foolish to accept ideas at face value. These are the individuals that quickly pour cold water on Face Pattern Recognition. They quickly make negative comments or form an opinion without having any in-depth know-how on how it works.

Many of the top football coaches have the Skeptical trait along with the Critical (outer corner of eye lower than inner corner) trait. They question and notice every move. Many of the top poker players also have this trait combination.

Famous Faces
Madeline Albright, Henry Kissinger, John Lennon

Relationships
If you have the Skeptical and Critical (outer corner of eye lower than inner corner) trait, try not to pour cold water on your partner's ideas by criticizing him or her. Make some suggestions and point out what he or she might consider or any precautions he or she should take. Be there to support him or her and your children.

Children
This trait is not developed until the teenage years, although children may well exhibit their skeptical nature with friends or family members. If you hear them being skeptical, you might point out how this could put a damper on their friends' ideas.

Sales
When you meet with Skeptical customers, be prepared to present all of the facts, more than what most of your clients need. If they are also Analytical (covered eyelid), be prepared for lots of questions.

Careers
Skeptical people make good judges, lawyers, financial planners, and athletic coaches, particularly for football or soccer.

The Trusting Nose

Upturned Nose
Very trusting

To determine if someone has an upturned nose, look at the nose from the side profile. When the nose angles up from the underside where it joins the lip, this indicates a more open-minded and trusting individual. However, people who are more trusting are often taken advantage of by others and may find themselves falling for other people's practical jokes or schemes. Many people with this facial feature have fallen under the spell of get-rich-quick ventures. Seldom do you see individuals with the Skeptical trait (down-turned nose) fall for the so-called business opportunities, better called "scams," now in abundance on the Internet.

Individuals with upturned noses have an almost childlike naiveté. They have a trusting and open nature and sorely want to believe in others. Even when they have fallen victim to some bad investment scheme, they still want to believe in the good of people. They are easily taken in by others and do not ask for proof before committing their hard-earned savings or time.

On the positive side, people with these facial features tend to be open-minded and receptive, willing to give something "a try." We see this trait in babies; however, if their parents have the Administrative (convex nose) trait, the child's nose shape will change during the later teenage years.

If you are a more Trusting individual, ask questions until you are *completely* satisfied before making a final commitment about a business venture. Do not be taken in by a "good deal." Ask someone who has knowledge about the product or opportunity for advice. Many Trusting and Impulsive (protruding lips) people have made purchases or investment they later regretted. They need to keep a little doubt in their minds.

The Trusting Nose

Famous People
Bob Hope, Elton John

Relationships
If they are the opposites in a relationship, the Trusting partner will feel their Skeptical partner does not support their ideas. However, if both partners have the Trusting trait, it would be a good idea for them to get a second opinion when they invest large amounts of money or time into a project or anything else for that matter.

Children
The Trusting trait is apparent in all children. This may change once they enter their teens. If the parents have this trait, then the child may well inherit a trusting nature as well.

Sales
When discussing a significant investment, you may want to make sure your Trusting client is not spending beyond their budget. Otherwise, you may be wasting your time. Show them a product or service that matches their budget, especially when investing in the real estate market.

Careers
This trait can be seen in all careers. If in a management position, that individual will need to delegate tasks out to one's fellow workers. This will be one of their challenges in a management position.

Self-Reliance

Flared Nostrils
Extremely independent

Self-Reliance constitutes an environmental trait determined by the flare of the nostrils. The larger the flare of the nostrils, the more self-reliant or independent the person becomes. However, the facial feature, and therefore, the trait changes according to the conditions surrounding the individual in their home and work environment. It also reflects one's own positive or negative inner chatter. The more determined an individual, the larger the nostrils flare.

High Self-Reliance people often insist on making decisions not only for themselves, but also for members of the family or for people with whom they work. They are used to doing things on their own and acting independently. They often feel their way represents the right way.

Many times people with the High Self-Reliance trait will take jobs away from other people because they feel they can do the work better and faster. They don't always trust others to do things correctly, and they get impatient when having to wait around for something they think they could have done in half the time.

The High Self-Reliant trait can be problematic when working with a team because people with this trait may not accept the authority of others. They have no idea how others react to their "do-it-on-my-own" attitude. Individuals with this trait need to stop and see what goes on around them, and they need to be more sensitive to the people whom they work with. They should stop and think about alternative ways of handling situations. For example, if a project is running behind, rather than take it away from the person handling it, the High Self-Reliant person might suggest working together to speed up the process. This avoids making the person handling the project, up until that point, feel unappreciated or perceived as incapable.

On the other hand, Low Self-Reliant individuals follow authority well, but they may relinquish their own authority too soon. They hesitate to do things by themselves, such as starting their own businesses. I knew a woman who had all of the qualifications and abilities to set up her own business, but as soon as she met an obstacle, she backed off. Despite several attempts to start a business without support from others, she found it difficult to move her ideas forward alone. Low Self-Reliant people don't feel comfortable working on their own. Their inner chatter—"I can't do it by myself." or "What if it doesn't work out?"—holds them back. If you find yourself repeating these thoughts to yourself, try using your mental "delete button," and replace it with positive thinking and action.

If an individual has extremely flared nostrils, they can be unforgiving; once you have crossed their path, they won't forget. They may hold whatever you have done against you for a lifetime. I observed this trait in a man in his early twenties. He acknowledged that he was very unforgiving, and that it posed a problem for him. He inquired how he could master this tendency. With coaching, he was able to move through the negative trait, and he gradually developed a technique for letting go of the past wrongs he felt had been done to him.

This was the case for a man who also had the flared nostrils and the Controlling trait (cupped out ears) also close-set eyes. Because his family would not take his side, in a fall out with his brother and his wife, he would have nothing more to do with them, despite many attempts on his family's part to heal the wounds. This included his children and grandchildren. This left the family members feeling sad, but nothing they could say or do made any difference to this man. Life is too short; one needs to learn to let go and heal the wounds.

Relationships

The partner who has the High Self-Reliance trait may take over and make all the decisions in a relationship, especially if the other partner takes too long to complete a project or making plans for a vacation. The High Self-Reliance individual will take over and do it his or her way, which could create some issues. If both the partners have this trait, they may well push each other emotionally away. Both will want to control the situation. If this is the case in your relationship, remind yourself to be more flexible and to go along with each other's suggestions or requests.

Children

If this trait develops in children, it indicates an independent nature. Parents may well find these children extremely challenging to raise.

Sales

Clients with the High Self-Reliance trait may get impatient if things are not moving along fast enough. If delays occur, reassure them all is well. Be aware that they may go somewhere else if progress is too slow.

Careers

This trait certainly serves as an asset when running your own business. It provides the determination that helps you get through the tougher times.

Chapter Six

The Eyebrows

Design Appreciation

An appreciation for how things are designed
Inverted V on top of the eyebrow

The eyebrows tell us much about a person. The high or low *placement* of the eyebrows indicates if an individual is more selective and formal or whether they come across as being more friendly and of a casual nature. The *shape* of the eyebrow indicates if an individual has a natural feel for the overall design of something. This could pertain to the design of a building, a garden, a Web site, a photograph, or a new project.

The Design Appreciation trait indicates an innate feel for how things are structured—the design of a building, the overall plans for a new business venture, the interior design of a space, or the design for an artistic creation. This trait is determined by the pyramid shape of the eyebrow, which is formed between the middle and outer edge of the eyebrow. Individuals with this innate ability have a sense of the overall structure of whatever interests them.

This trait is often observed in architects, designers, photographers, and entrepreneurs. They enjoy such activities as designing and organizing projects, conducting a meeting, or planning an event. They have a feel for how one element adds to another and how each part contributes to the total impression. Extremely conceptual by nature, they have a natural feel for the design before a project even has started. For this reason, they make great business architects; they often are successful in setting up and running new ventures, especially if they are Competitive (head wider at the back compared with the front) and have the Administrative (convex) nose.

Individuals with the Design Appreciation trait enjoy such activities as developing the groundwork for planning a housing development or creating a pleasing landscape. They can see where the project is going and can design the overall picture necessary for it to succeed. Combine Design Appreciation with Imagination (Mounds on the forehead) and Mechanical Appreciation (rounded eyebrows), and this trait cluster indicates the ability to plan and organize events, projects, or anything involving design and organization. Add the Perfectionist (outer corner of eye lower than inner corner) trait, and this adds to the person's ability to produce excellent results.

When we hired a contractor to rebuild our deck, I scrutinized each prospective contractor as they came in to give us a quote. The one with the most convex nose (Administrative) gave us the highest bid. The ski jump nose (Ministrative) with wide-set eyes (High Tolerance) never followed up, and the one with the close-set eyes (Low Tolerance) and Design Appreciation got the job. All of his workers had the Perfectionist (outer corner of the eye lower than the inner corner) trait. In the end, the workmanship was excellent. It was fascinating to watch them, as they painstakingly lined up each one of the railings and steps.

Design Appreciation

When the job was completed, I gave the contractor my book. He looked at me in surprise and said, "You hired me based on my face?" Indeed, I did, and if you are hiring someone to fix or repair something in your home or office, Face Pattern Recognition provides some added insight about the person you are hiring for the job. In addition to the references they give you, recognizing key traits in the face provides you with additional information about that person. For instance, you'll know if they are good with detail and if they see the problems that need to be fixed.

Famous Faces
Colin Powell, Simon Cowell, Mariska Hargitay

Relationships
In relationships, no issues exist with the Design Appreciation trait.

Children
Parents, if your children have the Design Appreciation trait, buy them toys that evoke their creative and design ability. Sign them up for classes that teach them how to improve their design skills. Keep a list of activities that seem to ignite their interest. This will provide a thread for you to refer to when the time comes to help them make career decisions.

Sales

If your client has the Design Appreciation trait, when appropriate, you might want to emphasize how well the product or service you sell is designed. This highlights the area of their interest, which could persuade them to a final decision.

Careers

People who have this trait enjoy careers, as well as hobbies, in photography, quilting, stained glass art, interior design Web site design, landscape architecture, graphic design and engineering. If they also have close-set eyes (Low Tolerance) they will enjoy designing and flying model airplanes.

Mechanical Appreciation

Mechanical Appreciation
The half-moon-shaped eyebrow

While Design Appreciation deals with how something is designed, Mechanical Appreciation involves bringing the parts together to make the whole.

When the eyebrows resemble the shape of a half-moon, this indicates a natural ability to bring things together. This includes assembling equipment, coordinating a project, organizing an event, or bringing a group of people together. People with the Mechanical Appreciation trait have extremely organized thoughts.

When people have both the Mechanical and Design Appreciation traits, they often enjoy careers such as event planners or interior designers. They have a natural gift to bring things together. Individuals with both of the above traits enjoy working where they can translate their innate feel of a situation into a finished project. If they also have an oval forehead (Conservation), they work well as project managers. Such people have a great sense of how to coordinate projects or events, and they have a real knack for "getting the gears to mesh."

Mechanical Appreciation

Disorganization can get these individuals down, especially if they have close-set eyes and tight skin (like to run things squeaky clean). If you enjoy having an organized system for your work and surroundings, and you aren't an organized individual, either hire someone to organize your office for you or develop a system that keeps your things in order. When you combine this trait with the Administrative, Acquisitive, and Competitive traits, these individuals are often successful fund raisers.

Famous Faces
Whitney Huston, Jennifer Aniston, George Clooney, Michelle Obama

Relationships

If your partner has the Mechanical Appreciation trait, you'll find yourself blessed with an organized home and a partner willing to organize trips and activities. If you tend to be more disorganized, your Mechanical Appreciation partner might find you a bit annoying at times.

Children

When parents see this trait in young children, they should buy them toys that engage their natural talent for design, such as Lego, puzzles, or Tinker Toys. They also can involve them in any activity where the children can design and assemble objects. Later, when the children are older, parents can encourage them to do computer graphics, stained glass art, quilting, or other art forms.

Sales

When working with a client who has the Mechanical Appreciation trait, you might want to point out how well the product or service you are selling has been assembled and the amount of thought put into developing it.

Careers

Suggested careers would include mechanical engineer, professional organizer, event planner, sound and lighting technician, fashion designer, flower arranger, architect, personal shopper, carpenter, or Web designer.

Dramatic Appreciation

The Dramatic Appreciation trait is indicated by the upward flair of the outer edges of the eyebrows. This trait is seen more easily in women, although a modified version of this trait is seen in many male movie stars and some top poker players. This trait indicates a love of drama. The world is a stage for these people. They have a natural flair for acting and a passion for the theater. This trait is often observed in people involved in the speaking profession as well. They are the natural performers. They put a lot more verbal and visual expression in their presentations.

I noticed this trait in some of the top poker players—the table becomes their stage. They can put on an act and fake the "tells" or moves. At the poker table or in "real life," people with the Dramatic Appreciation trait must face the challenge of not coming across as phony. I also noticed this trait in some of the top business women in England. Running a successful business is a way of setting the stage for them. It represents their success, and they enjoy the recognition that goes with it.

This dramatic flair can be seen in the way these individuals dress, how their homes are decorated, or in their work. It is expressed in their writing, painting, or any design-related project. They make presentations come alive.

If individuals with this trait enjoy writing, they will enjoy creating scripts for plays and movies. You often see this trait in event planners and caterers. It is an added talent that compliments their area of creative interest.

Individuals who have worked at a job for some time come to me because they seek a new career direction. My assessment often validates the career they are considering. This was the case for a sixty-five-year-old English lady who sent me her photograph for a career assessment. Based on her facial features, I thought she would excel in the theater and architecture. As it turned out, she had been interested in these areas as a teenager. She had often put on plays for her school. Later in life, she decided to take a course in architecture, but she gave up this pursuit because her husband was unhappy that the course meant she spent time away from being at home. So she dropped the course, and with it, her life's ambition.

As a child, I always wanted to be "on stage," and I would often put on plays for my family and friends at school. Acting represented an interest I wanted to pursue; however, this was not encouraged by my family. They probably saw my passion as a childhood fantasy. I did eventually get involved with some local operatic groups, and I thoroughly enjoyed myself. After we immigrated to Canada, I signed up to sing with a local musical group; it was great fun. Then we moved to Los Angeles. With no formal training, I did not have the nerve to audition for an acting part in a production; so much talent can be found in that area. Now many years later, one of the highlights of my work is speaking. It's my chance to get up on stage and perform.

I recently gave a workshop at AT&T. Ann, a deaf attendee, had two interpreters that took turns translating the information. One of them had the High Dramatic trait, which I mentioned to the deaf woman. She said that interpreter's dramatic gestures, which could be observed from his expression and use of his hands, gave greater meaning to what he was telling her. Apparently, most interpreters are less expressive. I felt quite excited about learning this from her. I had never really given much thought about how this natural dramatic ability would help deaf people.

Dramatic Appreciation

Ann loved the face reading workshop; she thought it was "cool." It gave her another tool to understand the people with whom she worked. Face pattern recognition is a great asset for the hearing impaired, especially when they meet someone for the first time. It would be useful for blind people too. They could listen for clues that can be heard in the quality of the person's voice and the way they express themselves. For instance, a soft voice would indicate fine hair and the Sensitive trait. If they sound "bottom line," they would know that person is more action-driven.

Famous Faces
Halle Berry, Tom Cruise, Michelle Obama

Relationships
If you are more dramatic, your partner may see you as overreacting to situations and taking them out of context. On the positive side, find plays or musicals that you both will both enjoy. This also could include attending art or photography exhibits or any event that includes drama. If you both have the Risk-Taking traits (ring finger longer than index finger), activities such as car racing or any sporting event will be enjoyable to pursue together.

Children

If you are the parent of a child with the Dramatic Appreciation trait, sign them up for children's theater classes or any activity that puts them "on stage." This also includes sports, dance, art class, gymnastics, and ice skating, or any other activity that offers an outlet for their creative ability. If children have this trait and do not get the attention needed, they may well do or say things to become the center of attention in other ways. Praise and recognize your children for what they have achieved no matter how significant that is.

Sales

Clients with the Dramatic Appreciation trait are more expressive and creative. For such clients, you might want to put emphasis in your presentation on creative elements to give it more dramatic impact.

Careers

People with this trait enjoy teaching, lecturing, professional athletics, event planning, acting, performing, catering, art, or any career where the job puts them "on stage."

Aesthetic Appreciation

Underside of Eyebrow Straight
An appreciation for balance and harmony

When the underside of the eyebrow is straight, horizontal, or flat, this indicates the presence of heightened Aesthetic Appreciation. This trait indicates the degree to which a person is moved by the impression one receives through one's feelings. These High Aesthetic Appreciation individuals have a great sense of balance and harmony, and they enjoy being surrounded by beautiful things. This does not necessarily indicate that one has artistic ability, however. One can have great appreciation for beautiful things without having an innate ability to produce them.

You can see this trait in a number of the more popular male movie stars and male models. It can be harder to see this in women because they pluck their eyebrows. Certainly, it can be identified in children.

High Aesthetic Appreciation individuals have strong feelings and appreciation of their surroundings, and they tend to do things that make the environment better for everyone. They rarely raise their voices or make "emotional waves." If unpleasantness occurs, they do their best to manage it equitably for all concerned—unless there is a clash of values.

These people love nature and feel at one with the elements. They have a real sense of the harmony of things, whether they see it in nature, a painting, the way a building is designed, or the flow of a piece of music. Many famous artists and musicians have the Aesthetic Appreciation trait.

When the Aesthetic Appreciation individuals' lives fall out of balance, they may get caught up in a vicious cycle of turning to what makes them feel good. In other words, they try to satisfy their need for balance and harmony to dull the discord in their lives. They want to escape from what irritates them and may run away from problems instead of facing and solving them. These are intense individuals; they pour themselves into anything they are passionate about to the point of obsession.

Many of these individuals want to contribute to an environmental or humanitarian cause. This stems from their desire to create balance throughout the world. Barack Obama has this trait.

If you're a High Aesthetic Appreciation individual, your challenge lies in identifying and dealing with the situations that cause the imbalance in your life. You need to take responsibility for creating your own harmony, and you need to stop expecting anyone else to do it for you. Don't try to escape the imbalance through alcohol, drugs, or anything else that gives only temporary release. Be careful not to let pleasing things and pleasurable sensations distract you. Learn how to create and to leave the world with something worthwhile and lasting.

Aesthetic Appreciation

If you find yourself out of balance, sign up for a yoga class. Include meditation as a part of your daily activity. If these things are not possible, develop a plan to get your life back on track. Hire a personal coach to support and encourage you through your challenges.

Famous Faces
Mel Gibson, Russell Crowe

Relationships
If your partner has this trait and he or she is under a lot of stress at work, suggest taking some time off. Even if it just means going for a short walk, recommend to the High Aesthetic Appreciation individual to engage in any activity that may help him or her get his or her life back in balance.

Children
When school or home situations are more challenging, High Aesthetic Appreciation children may become stressed out. Find out what is going on and suggest an activity that helps them relax. You might ask them if they would like to sign up for an art or music class. This will help them relax during the more stressful moments in their lives.

Sales
If your client has this trait, he or she will be sensitive to how the product you are selling is put together. Or if you work in real estate, the client will be more interested in homes featuring designs with a natural flow. Some people may call this feng shui, which focuses on how the design flows together and has balance.

Careers

Individuals who have the Aesthetic Appreciation trait should consider becoming artists, designers, musicians, naturalist, collectors, and environmentalists. Their artistic interests could also be a hobby,

Affable/Discriminating

Affable
Low-set eyebrows

Discriminating
High-set eyebrows

The Affable and Discriminating traits reflect the timing of·a person's response to situations going on in the moment. If the eyebrow is high-set that person tends to be more selective in their decision-making and thinking responses, whereas, the person with low-set eyebrows tends to move in on things and act right away.

Two female professors with backgrounds in international affairs were asked what action other countries would take regarding the peace plan being negotiated in Israel. The person with the high-set eyebrows (Discriminating) stated, "I think they will wait to see how the situation develops." The person with the low-set eyebrows (Affable) stated, "Oh, I believe other countries will follow their path." The first professor wanted to survey the situation first, which reflected her Discriminating trait. The other woman, who was more Affable, thought other countries would react quickly, which reflected her "Let's-move-in-now" attitude.

Discriminating: More Selective

This trait is determined by the height of the eyebrow in comparison to the vertical height of the eye aperture. When the distance between the top of the eyelid to the bottom of the eyebrow is greater than the vertical height of the eye, this trait indicates a person is more Discriminating or selective and comes across as being more formal. On the other hand, a person with low-set eyebrows is generally more casual.

In the Western world, low-set eyebrows (Affable) tend to be a male-dominant trait, whereas the high-set eyebrows (Discriminating) tend to be a female-dominant trait. Most people of Asian heritage have high-set eyebrows. The studies conducted by Jones, found that people with high-set eyebrows, regardless of culture, tend to behave in a more formal manner. Once you get to know them, however, they show their friendly side. When you meet these people, shake hands and go through all the formalities. Then let them make the first move.

Individuals with high-set eyebrows are more select about the friends they make as well as their purchases and decisions. Don't try to rush them into the latter. When shopping for clothes, it may take them a long time before they make a final purchase. They are not impulse buyers. They would rather leave without buying anything, rather than purchase something that's not totally satisfactory. They like to make sure they have made the right decision before making the final purchase. When they make friends, they do so for a lifetime.

When meeting people with high-set eyebrows, step up, shake hands, then step back, and allow four to five feet between the two of you, unless they initiate closer contact. When conducting a meeting around a table with individuals who have this trait, do not place your elbow on the table or lean toward them, unless you know them well enough to do so. Make an effort to put them at ease, and show them you are interested in them as individuals, but give them "formal" space. Don't treat them informally, unless you have already established a friendship or client relationship.

Discriminating

Since Discriminating people may appear to be more reserved and less friendly, this builds psychological barriers. Others may perceive them as being aloof or less approachable. This is not their intention. Many people with this trait have expressed that they feel lonely. They wonder why people do not readily approach them. I saw a woman with this trait at a workshop I attended. She spent much of the day on her own. Noticing this, I went over and spoke to her. She looked at me in surprise, and she told me she usually had to make the first move to strike up a conversation with someone. She always felt she was a very approachable person, and she could not understand why people did not come up to her.

I have noticed that people in the United States tend to abbreviate the names of people they meet without first checking to ask what that person likes to be called. For instance, a person may introduce himself as "Anthony," and his name is immediately abbreviated to "Tony." Check with him first before you abbreviate his name. A Discriminating person could take offense at this "informal" use of his name. If you are a salesperson, don't lose a potential client by shortening his or her name.

Appearing too formal is often perceived as being less approachable. If you have this Discriminating trait, make an effort to break down the unseen barrier. Wear softer colors or prints; this helps soften the formality, and you will be seen as more approachable.

Affable

Individuals with low-set eyebrows make friends easily and quickly show interest in what is happening around them. They like to make physical contact, such as giving someone a light touch on the shoulder, arm, or even the knee, and sometimes, offering a hug. If they move in too close and too fast, they risk taking more Discriminating people by surprise. If you are an Affable individual, know when this approach is appropriate and when it is not. Your challenge comes in honoring other people's space.

Affable

Individuals with low-set eyebrows have a more casual approach to most things, and they often come across as your old friend or buddy. They also move in and out of situations quickly, which can seem confusing to the person they have just met. They exchange business cards or phone numbers with the promise to call. Affable people see such gestures as casual contact, however, and feel they have offered no promise to pursue these relationships. The person they have just met, however, might mistakenly think they just made a new friend, and is surprised when no follow up occurs. Often I hear, "I thought this was a new friend...I really liked her." There's a feeling of being let down or disappointed by the Affable individuals they encounter. If you have this trait, make it known to those you meet that you perceive this as a casual encounter with no expectations.

Famous Faces: Selective
Hilary Clinton, Diane Sawyer

Famous Faces: Affable
Tom Cruise, Simon Cowell, George Clooney

Relationships
The Affable trait combined with Magnetism (sparkling eyes) can often send out the wrong message to people of the opposite sex. Others will see them as being flirtatious. Their partner may become jealous because they may think an affair is beginning.

Children

Children with the Discriminating trait (high-set eyebrows) may appear to be less friendly or even shy. It may take them a while to make friends, whereas, Affable children will find it very easy to make friends.

Sales

If you meet with a client who has high-set eyebrows, behave a little more formally. Do not move into their space too soon, or they will back away. Don't reach out and make any physical contact, or your Discriminating client will see you as acting in too familiar a manner. Although this may not be your intent, it could put them off.

Careers

There are no specific careers for this trait.

CHAPTER SEVEN

THE HEAD

Confidence

Narrow Face
Builds confidence

Wide Face
High self-confidence

An individual's degree of self-confidence is determined by the width of the face, which is measured from the outer edge of one eyebrow to the outer edge of the other eyebrow, compared with the length of the face from the chin to the turn of the forehead. A special tool was designed to accurately determine the width of the left and right sides of the face, since they are not always the same. This determines if one side of the face is narrower compared with the other. If so, this indicates that sometimes that individual feels more confident and other times less confident.

Self-confidence is a feeling, not an intellectual awareness of one's potential. In other words, innate self-confidence constitutes how the individual feels about himself or herself. Individuals who have wide faces feel confident and self-assured in the face of challenges or environmental circumstances. They assume they can take on anything whether or not they have the knowledge or experience, whereas, a narrow-faced individual feels extremely hesitant when faced with new situations.

Narrow Face

Individuals with narrow faces build their confidence through knowledge and experience. They take class after class just to make sure they have enough information to start their new business or career. They build a strong foundation of knowledge.

A bright narrow-faced engineer who was well known for his expertise in his field was asked to give a presentation to some prominent engineers in Germany. This represented the first time he had given a presentation to such a distinguished group. When the time came to present his paper, he felt terrified and fumbled through the presentation. The tension inside him seemed agonizing. He left feeling he had not met the group's expectations. The whole experience devastated him.

If his employers had prepared him beforehand, he could have given a successful presentation. His manager might have said to him, "This is new for you. Here is someone you can work with to help you prepare the talk." This approach would have removed much of the fear from the presentation.

Many employees complain that their employers do not offer enough training or support for people who are facing new situations or positions in the company. This is particularly true for narrow-faced people who feel the need to know more to feel comfortable compared with wide-faced people who have more self-confidence. Many employees with narrow faces have walked off their jobs because the thought of facing new situations with no support in place seemed too daunting. If managers just took the time to put in place a training program, it would save the company far more than the cost of the training.

Narrow Face

Whereas, the wide-faced, or High Self-Confidence person is self-assured, the narrow-faced person finds unfamiliar tasks or situations beyond their realm of expertise overwhelming. People with narrow faces are intensely aware of their limitations and, consequently, more apt to stay with what feels familiar or comfortable, rather than striking out boldly in new fields. This depends on other facial features, or traits, that may support or diminish self-confidence. To rise above discouragement, they need to have some real incentive or a goal. Otherwise, these individuals risk surrendering to self-doubt and old fear-oriented reactions, especially when confronted with wide-faced individuals, new situations, or challenges.

If you have a narrow face and can relate to being hesitant in new situations, think about the times when you have pulled through before, despite your feelings of uncertainty. Keep in mind that fear stems from your lack of information and experience. Remind yourself that you can achieve both.

Low self-esteem is often seen in people with narrow faces and close-set eyes (Low Tolerance). If these people are raised in nonsupportive environments, it takes quite some time before they believe in themselves. Add Critical Perception (outer corner of the eye lower than the inner corner) to the above trait cluster, and this really can impact their self-esteem.

One woman I met who had close-set eyes (Low Tolerance) and a narrow face, felt extremely fearful of stepping out of her secure life. She did not need to work, yet she had the desire to find her own niche in life. Fear held her back. With some coaching, she was able to move her life forward and work through the fear.

If you have the trait cluster of close-set eyes and narrow face, focus on what you want to bring into your life. We often wish for things to happen so much that I think we tend to hold on to our desires too tightly. The anxiety we feel about the possibility of our dreams not manifesting keeps us from moving towards our goals. Catch yourself when you go into the anxiety mode, which is often experienced by individuals who have the above trait cluster. Spend a couple of minutes each day thinking about what you would like to manifest in your life. Just let the thoughts go without any expectation. This technique has worked for many of my clients. Focus on the possibilities, not the obstacles.

Individuals with narrow faces are willing to stand back and learn from others and evaluate situations. They are aware of their own limitations. Once they gain knowledge in their field, they have all the confidence in the world. Until they have the knowledge needed, they are unlikely to confront the world. For this reason, people with narrow faces will appear to others as hesitating before taking on anything new. Often times, these individuals presume their inadequacy. Notice I avoid using the term "low self-confidence" when describing narrow-faced people. People hang on to this label, and it keeps their lives on hold. Hence, using "builds confidence through knowledge" seems a better way to describe their perception of themselves or how they approach life.

Other traits such as Forcefulness (head higher at the back) and High Competitive (head wider at the back compared with the front) make narrow-faced people appear more confident than they actually feel inside. These traits combined with Risk Taking (ring finger longer than the index finger) tend to push these people out on the edge. This trait cluster keeps them wondering why they keep putting themselves in such challenging situations.

If you have a narrow-face and you are going for a job interview, networking at an event, or giving a presentation, wear darker colors, such as black, navy, deep green, deep purple, or red. These are "power colors" that will support your verbal and your visual message. If you wear lighter colors at these events people may not take you quite as seriously, and you will have to work harder to get your message across.

If you are at all hesitant about speaking in front of an audience, or simply standing up and giving a two-minute pitch or introduction at meetings, you might want to take a speaking class. This will help you overcome your fear of speaking. An organization called Speaking Circles has a very good program.

On the positive side of this trait, individuals with a narrow face are aware of their limitations, and they are quick to seek out others or take classes to enhance their knowledge.

However, individuals with this trait tend to undersell themselves. Rather than fight pressure, they may conform or run away from it. They may feel inadequate because they lack either experience or knowledge needed to take on a new task. Once they have the knowledge, the situation will seem less daunting. They'll have all the confidence necessary to succeed.

Famous Faces
Tennis player Novak Djokovic, Andy Murray, Jennifer Aniston, Julia Roberts, tennis player Maria Sharapova

Relationships
Be there to support your narrow-faced partner in new situations. Get them to relax when they appear to be overly anxious.

Children
Often, children with narrow faces are extremely hesitant about meeting new people. Their parents' term this behavior as "shy." The child may take that label into their adult life. We often hear adults say, "I'm very shy at parties or networking events." In fact, they may just be hesitant, but they have adopted the term given them at an early age.

Narrow-faced children need exposure to all kinds of experiences, under supervision, in small doses. Allow them to take just one step at a time. Once the children have a basic knowledge of what to expect, they will have the ability to handle the new situation easily.

Parents need to support and acknowledge their children's achievements whether small or large. If children with narrow faces are also Sequential Thinkers (linear forehead) parents shouldn't hurry them or try to skip educational levels. It's best to let these children grow and learn at their own pace. Parents should give them new assignments one at a time, and make sure they understand each step before they move on to the next.

If your child appears to be hesitant in new situations, be there to support them. Don't just say, "You'll be fine." Talk them through the situation and explain what they will experience. If they dread an exam, especially if they have the Sequential Thinking (vertical forehead) trait, which indicates they do not do well under pressure, help them relax beforehand. Play music in the background, this will help them to relax.

Sales

Be there to support your narrow-faced customers. Make sure they really understand how to use the new tool or service you are offering. When possible, follow up with a phone call to answer any questions that may have come up.

Careers

There are no specific careers for individuals with narrow faces, although this trait is often seen in teachers, coaches, accountants, therapists, health-related fields, plus many more.

Wide Face

We often see the High Self-Confidence trait in many leaders, such as Winston Churchill, Edward Kennedy, Oprah Winfrey, and Hilary Clinton. These people enjoy a leading role in life. It would be hard for them to stay in the background and play a supportive role, especially if they have a Roman nose (Administrative). This trait cluster is typical of people who'd like to be in charge. If they have a ski-jump nose (Ministrative), their leadership will take on a softer and gentler message.

Wide-faced people only feel challenged when they take on extremely large responsibilities or new projects. However, this is a feeling—not necessarily a fact. As one wide-faced person shared with me, "I fake it 'til I make it." It never occurred to her that she didn't have enough experience or information to take on the new project. She felt comfortable learning on the job.

High Self-confidence people look as though they are in charge. You can spot them as soon as you enter a room because they radiate self-assurance. Even though they may not be talking to you, you can feel they are people to be reckoned with. When they speak, their voices come across as being more assertive. They take command of a situation. When confronted or challenged by others, they raise the volume of their voice to be in control.

Wide Face

When they wear more formal colors, such as black or navy, this re-enforces their presence to the point where they can be extremely intimidating. If you have a wide face, wear softer colors when in meetings with fellow co-workers. Otherwise, they may not participate for fear of being judged by you.

The High Self-Confidence person needs to learn that problems come with power. Just because they feel self-assured doesn't make them right in what they want. If you have this trait, learn to be a leader who works with and for people. Become an inspiration to your followers.

Famous Faces

Edward Kennedy, Andre Agassi, Diane Sawyer, Martha Stewart

Relationships

If the two people in a relationship have a similar width of face, chances are they will be more compatible. If the differences in facial features are significant, what each partner at first liked in the other will become an irritation later. The wide-faced (High Self-Confidence) individual will come across as being more dominant, and in some cases crush their partner's confidence. They'll want to call the shots. Advice to High Self-Confidence partners: Be supportive and keep silent about what you think your partner ought to do—at least until asked. When needed, offer constructive advice or suggestions. Be there to support your partner.

The narrow-faced person in a relationship may feel their High Self-Confidence partner has no faith in them. In such cases, they feel all their decisions are being made for them, and they are forced into doing things they would rather not do. Narrow-faced people feel unappreciated for what they do and not respected for who they are. When wide-faced (High Self-Confidence) people laugh at the little things that please or upset their narrow-faced partners, the narrow-faced person will feel their partners are trying to put them down, and then they feel bad. This makes it harder for them to speak up because they feel they will be ridiculed.

If you are more self-confident, support the growth and creativity of those who tend to feel less confident. When you work with someone with a narrow face, recognize that person needs to be familiar with new situations first. Be prepared to support them.

Children

When working with wide-faced children, parents need to be more assertive, especially if the parent has a narrow face. Otherwise, when the children become teenagers, the parents may have problems coping with their children's control and discipline issues. The parents need to be consistent in how they raise their High Self-Confidence children, and they need to be supportive of each other as well.

Wide-faced children must be willing to take directions and do so cheerfully from people in authority. They need to learn to accept supervision gracefully and to become good followers. This will later help them become good leaders.

Sales

If you have a narrow face and your client has the High Self Confidence trait, make sure you wear darker colors that support your verbal and visual message. Use a strong voice and positive body language. Don't be intimidated by the wide-faced customer.

Careers

This trait is found in all careers. It does not limit a person's career choices.

TO CONSERVE

Oval Forehead

The maintainer

TO CONSTRUCT

Square Forehead

Likes to start new things

The tendency to either preserve and save what one has created or obtained, as opposed to engaging in new projects and letting go of old things, can be determined by the shape of the forehead following the hairline. To determine this facial feature, notice if the head in this area looks oval or square. To better understand where to look for the curve, look at the area just under the hairline on the sketch. If rounded, this indicates the person has the oval-forehead, we call this trait Conservation.

High Conservation: Oval Forehead

High Conservation people are good at maintaining projects and see things through to the end. They like to preserve what they already have. They hold on to things just in case they will be useful another day. If this trait is combined with High Acquisitiveness (protruding ears), these people can be "pack rats" or hoarders. Unlike individuals with square foreheads (Construction), they have a hard time throwing things out. They hold on to their possessions for years, including screws, small pieces of wood, paper with outdated information, and old magazines. To others, this looks like "junk" collecting dust; roommates or spouses may perceive the items as having no further value and actually throw them out. If you are guilty of throwing other people's things out, perhaps you should first ask what the other person would like to keep, especially if these things belong to children. You may have no idea if an item is of value to that person, especially if they have an oval forehead (High Conservation).

The High Conservation individual places a lot of importance on home and family. Their home and family means everything to them. They love to fix up old things, remodel the house, and rearrange the furniture.

Individuals with this trait like to nurture. When combined with the Growing Trend (large ear lobes), this individual may enjoy gardening. This trait cluster is often seen in people who work in the hotel industry, hospitals, and healthcare. It also can be observed in dieticians, chemists, psychologists, chefs, and project managers, as well as in any career focused on maintaining or preserving something. These traits prove beneficial in sales or customer service too. These individuals are great at maintaining client relationships.

Conserve: Oval Forehead

High Conservation individuals love to work out at gyms or participate in any other activities on a regular basis. They stay with the same job for years. If they are less adventurous, some will never travel outside of their town. To the Construction person and the more adventurous, this seems really boring.

Famous Faces
Tom Hanks, John Cleese, Andrew Lloyd Webber, Halle Berry, Martha Stewart

Relationships
If you have the High Conservation trait and your partner has the High Construction trait (square forehead), be more open to visiting new places, rather than going on the same walk every day, to the same restaurant, or to the same place on vacation. Create some variety, and then your partner will be more eager to go on trips and participate in different activities.

Children
Children who have the High Conservation trait keep their friends over long periods of time. They won't like to throw things away; their possessions are important to them.

Sales
If you work in the real estate business and your client has the High Conservation trait, he or she won't mind buying a house that needs remodeling.

Careers

High Conservation individuals do well in careers that involve counseling, teaching, electronic engineering, botany, and catering, as well as in jobs in medical and health related-fields.

High Construction: Square Forehead

Individuals with square foreheads (High Construction) go to the gym a couple of times and then drop out. They don't like doing things on a regular basis, unless they feel really passionate about the activity, or it is needed to improve their skills. They don't like repetition. They like new things! They want to start projects from scratch rather than re-model. They are less likely to hang on to things that could be useful another day. They don't like clutter, and often, they throw items out that could be useful one day. Their philosophy is simple: If I need something in the future, I can always go out and purchase it again. They like to throw things out and start afresh. This appears wasteful to people with the High Conservation trait.

Construction: Square
Forehead

Once the High Construction person has done something, it's finished. "Been there, done that" is their motto. They find it extremely boring to maintain a project for a long period of time; this also applies to client relationships. They see a client a few times, and then they want them to go on their merry way. They lose interest in anything that repeats itself too often. They find going on the same walk, doing the same thing day after day, or anything that has routine will be boring. For this reason, they make many career changes throughout their lives. If their career offers a lot of different activities, they are more likely to stay with it over time.

High Construction people tune in to whatever's new. They love to start new projects, come up with new ideas, and move to new locations. When they focus on new projects, they put all their energy and time into developing them or getting them off the ground. All else fades into the background; they resent being pulled away from their projects to attend to less interesting activities.

The challenging aspect of this trait lies in the fact that these individuals do not hold on to something in case it could be useful later. They also don't make do with what they already have. They are inclined to spare no expense to have the "new" when the "old" would serve just as well.

If you have a square forehead, learn to "make-do" with what is already available, rather than rushing out and getting something new. When you find yourself saying, "Let's start from scratch," stop and check to see what is on hand that would serve to begin your project.

Individuals with this trait tend to be overly absorbed in their careers, often to the point where they neglect themselves and their families. For example, this became a problem for a young couple and their children. Their father who had the High

Construction trait was never home, and his children saw little of him as they were growing up. He was constantly at work, spending very little time with his wife or children. For him, to take time out from his job was an interruption. After a consultation with me, the husband agreed to set aside some time each week, for the family to have quality time together.

Women with this trait will find staying at home boring. They need to fill their days with a part-time job. If they have a mixture of both Conservation (oval forehead) and Construction, this will indicate that sometimes they will want to stay at home, while the other side would like to be working. Working out of the home represents an ideal situation for these people.

The idea of retirement does not appeal to people who have the High Construction trait. The mere thought of it seems scary to them. They can't imagine what they will do with all of that time. They need to have a purpose in life, or they quickly get bored. Networking or volunteering does not appeal to them either; they go a couple of times and then drop out. However, if a meeting offers something new each time, they more than likely will attend. These people enjoy going to workshops just for the pure enjoyment of learning something new. They may not do anything with the new knowledge, they are life-long students.

Because they let their careers dominate their lives, High Construction types need to pay attention to the "creature comforts." They must meet their own basic needs and the needs of their families, as well as attending to their own health. They need to schedule time for family and close friends. Additionally, they need to recognize that life does not have to be all about work. If you are one of these people, schedule some time to play.

This trait is often seen in marketing professionals. They are the seed planters, the people with new ideas. They develop and launch their ideas and then move on to the next project. Often, they feel confused by this tendency within themselves, especially since to others, it appears as inconsistency or a lack of "stick-to-it-ness." When I gave a workshop to the IBM marketing division, I noticed that at least 90 percent of the people from that department had this trait. They like to plant the ideas and get the salespeople to follow through.

I remember standing in a shop doorway, speaking to someone who had just flown over from England. I had noticed her square forehead and explained to her that she would change her career many times. Later, she told me, she felt a sense of great relief when she heard my words. Until that time, she couldn't understand why she was not more like her friends, who stayed in one job for a long time. After my quick assessment, for the first time, she understood that side of herself, that aspect of her personality.

Famous Face
Barack Obama

Relationships

When opposite personality traits exist in a relationship, the partner who has the Conservation trait will find their Construction partner extremely bored by visiting the same place over and over again. "But we've been there already," the Construction partner will say. The Conservation partner will respond, "Yes, but I love to go there again. I find it fascinating." The Construction partner will still want to go somewhere else, even if it's just for a walk; for this person, the destination will have to be different each time.

If you have the High Construction trait, be flexible and go back to the same place with your High Conservation partner. Share their enjoyment. If you have the Conservation trait, remember that change is good now and again. Your partner is not trying to be awkward or annoying. They just want to do something different. Both people in the relationship should be flexible to each other's needs and preferences.

Children

Parents are often confused when their children seem to lose interest in activities, for which they have signed them up, be it learning to play a musical instrument, playing a sport, or taking an art class. The student seems to excel in the class or sports, and the teachers see someone who is talented and has the potential to do well in that activity. Then all of a sudden, the child or teenager decides to drop out. This confuses the coach or teacher because they see someone who has the ability to do extremely well. However, this represents typical behavior for square-headed students. Even in their studies at school, repeating the same old thing over and over again quickly bores them. Many a teenager drops out of school or college because they have no idea what direction to pursue. Having tried many different classes, nothing seems to hold their interest. This is typical of a High Construction personality.

Having worked with a number of students, I have found that once they understand the trait and have a career direction that ignites their interest, they generally stay enrolled in college. They just need to find a career that offers them many different activities. Generally, psychology does not hold their interest even though they have the abilities to match that career. It will bore them to meet with their clients over and over again. Many psychologists with the High Construction trait have shared with me that they breathe a sigh of relief when they cut back the times they see their clients.

Career counseling would probably work better because they don't have to meet with their clients as often.

Sales

If you work in real estate, clients with the Construction trait will not be interested in remodeling or repairing a home. They will be more interested in a home that is ready to move into or needs only minor repairs or changes. If you are selling a product or service, you might want to emphasize how this will add to what your High Construction client is already doing.

Careers

People who have the Construction trait tend to do well in jobs that involve marketing, teaching workshops, product development, or any career that offers a variety of activities.

Thinking Style

Objective Thinker
Sloped Back Forehead

Sequential Thinker
Vertical Forehead

Sally, a Sequential Thinker (vertical forehead), told me she feels "thrown off" at work when a plan has been made and is suddenly changed. She likes to stick with what was previously agreed upon. If that isn't possible, it works better for her if the other person making the change asks, "What do you think about this?" This helps her become more flexible and counter her automatic "no." Or if someone says, "Here's another way to look at it," this also makes her more receptive to change. When a chattering coworker interrupts Sally, she feels annoyed and becomes quickly rattled. If, however, that person says, "Can I talk to you for a minute?" that produces a better response than just interrupting her when she is in the middle of doing something, such as working on the computer.

To determine if someone has a vertical forehead (Sequential Thinker), look at the side profile of their head. Does the angle of the forehead slope backward or is it vertical? If it slopes backward, this individual is an Objective Thinker, quick to think and respond in the moment. If the forehead is straight up and down, this person is a Sequential Thinker and prefers a step-by-step approach.

The various "thinking" traits have to do with how people process information, not what they think about, or the quality or quantity of their thoughts. Objective Thinkers are inclined to allow their automatic reactions, based on present or past experiences, to determine their thoughts in the moment. Sequential Thinkers are inclined to consciously process "new" ideas or challenges through a rational and logical thought process. In other words, Objective Thinkers deal in reactions to something, and Subjective Thinkers deal with the "thing or situation" itself.

Sequential Thinkers: Vertical Forehead

Sequential Thinkers are turned off by fast "high pressure" sales or tactics. They need time to examine each step of the process. If they miss part of the information due to rapid delivery, they get lost and the subsequent information goes over their heads. Once they understand the missing piece, however, everything becomes clear. Under pressure, their minds may go blank, particularly during exams or if a test is suddenly presented to them; they know the answers but their minds freeze. Whether it is a last-minute test or a response to an emergency situation, they need time to think through their decisions. At times, Sequential Thinkers find it difficult to "speed up" mentally.

When interacting with Sequential Thinkers, check to make sure they have understood the information you have covered before going on to the next step. Give them time to assimilate the new information. When appropriate, hand them a written outline so they can follow or review the information ahead of time. When possible, offer a general review at the end.

If a Sequential-Thinking person asks you for help in performing some task, make sure you explain the basic steps that lead up to the solution, or this person will become completely lost by any additional instruction. If people with this trait haven't understood a previous point, they shut down in frustration, and they won't hear what is being said. Give them all the steps needed before moving on.

Remember, this trait has nothing to do with intellect; it is related to how this person processes information. They need to go step-by-step. For example, when you are giving Sequential Thinkers instructions on how to use the computer or a computer program, make sure they understand the first steps. Otherwise, if you do not establish that they know how to get to B without first explaining A, they will become completely lost.

Sequential Thinkers like to get to their destinations and appointments in plenty of time. If they are unexpectedly delayed, they feel rushed and experience a high sense of anxiety about possibly not arriving on time. Typically, they like to arrive at the airport two hours ahead of time. If they run late, they become very anxious. They need to let their traveling companions know they would like to leave by a specific time. If you have this trait, just explain that it makes you feel more relaxed if you leave on time. This takes off the pressure, and you won't feel as stressed.

To the Objective Thinker, Sequential Thinkers appear to be very slow. Sometimes, when the Sequential Thinker is asked a question, they mull things over in

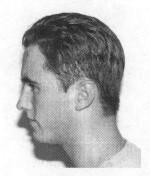

Sequential Thinker

their heads before responding. This can be annoying to the person with the opposite trait, who will attempt to hurry them up by saying, "What's taking you so long to respond?"

The Sequential Thinker also has the tendency to start a conversation in the middle of a thought; the other person won't have a clue what they're talking about. A school principal with this trait experienced this challenge when he first took up his new position. He said he would begin speaking, and people would look at him with blank stares. He quickly learned to start speaking at the beginning of his thought.

Many students with this trait find taking exams or tests very stressful. They know the work, but their mind goes blank under pressure. Many a student with this trait has been labeled a slow learner, which is often not the case.

A Swedish woman who had heard about my work suggested to her niece, who lived in Poland, that she send her photos to me for a career assessment. Her niece, who was in her last year at school, was feeling depressed and experiencing a low point in her life. She dreaded exam time because it felt like such a struggle for her. I found it easy to spot her vertical forehead in the photo. After she received her chart and listening to the CD I sent her with my assessment, she understood herself much better, and she knew how to approach exam time. Knowing her thinking style helped her get the best results she had ever achieved in school, and she later signed up for Warsaw University. Her parents were amazed and said, "All that from reading her face?"

Our face gives us clues as to why we behave and think the way we do, clues that have simply been ignored in most cases, yet they are staring us in the face. Can you imagine the difference it would make if teachers and parents were able to identify these traits in their children? I strongly believe that if more teachers knew about this face analysis system, their knowledge would be reflected in their students' academic scores at the end of the year.

Famous Faces

Tennis player Lindsay Davenport

Most of your professional sports players will have the Objective Thinking trait along with the politicians. Their sport or work often requires them to immediately react to situations and to "think on their feet."

Relationships

If you make plans to go somewhere on Saturday morning, and then when the day arrives, you change your mind, you might want to warn your Sequential Thinking partner ahead of time. This helps them be more flexible. If you're going to interrupt them when they are at the computer, go in and say "When you have a moment . . ." and leave the room. If you ask them a question, and they seem to be taking their time to answer—or you wonder if they heard you, be patient, they are thinking through the process.

Children

The Sequential-Thinking trait is often a challenge for children in school because they appear to be slow learners and are misunderstood. Many children with this trait are also accused of not concentrating because they don't hear what is said.

This was the case for Steve, a twelve-year-old boy who had the vertical forehead. His teacher thought he had a learning disability and recommended he go into a special English class for slow learners. In order for Steve to stay in the class, the school requested his parents come in and meet with the school psychologist. The first words the school psychologist said to the parents were, "What is Steve doing in this class? He is writing at college level."

Steve's Sequential style of learning had been misunderstood by his teacher. If she had recognized his preferred learning style, she would not have recommended the special class. There must be hundreds if not thousands of children who have experienced this frustration. Hopefully, teachers or parents reading this section will be able to understand and work with children who have this trait.

If your child or student has the Sequential Thinking trait, make sure their questions are answered or that they fully understand the instructions. If you change your plans for the day, give them plenty of warning. If a last-minute change occurs, discuss with them the reasons for the change; this will help them change gears.

As parents, you need to let your children's teachers know that they have this trait. This will avoid some of the frustration they experience in school. If your children have problems taking exams, suggest they play music in their heads while they are studying for exams or taking tests; this will help them relax. If the teacher were to play soft music in the classroom during exam time, it would help to relax the student. Many a student I have worked with who struggled in exam time, all are now at the top of their class. They experience a new level of confidence, which is reflected in their test results.

Sales

As mentioned, Sequential Thinkers are turned off by high pressure sales or tactics. If you find yourself selling to someone with a vertical forehead, explain the service, product, or document to your customer step-by-step. Make sure they have completely understood everything before you move on to something new. Don't start in the middle, or they will be lost. Give the client with the Sequential Thinking trait time to respond and think things through. Don't rush them into making a commitment or you may lose the order. Ask them if they need some time to think things over before making a decision. This approach will take away the sales pressure and make them more inclined to buy right away. If you try to pressure them into making a decision right there and then, chances are they will walk away.

Careers

No specific careers exist for individuals with the Sequential Thinking trait. They make great teachers or workshop presenters because they deliver instructions and information in a step-by-step manner. This makes it easier for their students to follow what is being taught.

The Objective Thinker: Sloped-back forehead

Objective Thinkers are quick decision-makers and often jump to conclusions or "second-guess" what other people are going to say or do before getting all the information. They instantly respond to what is going on around them, and often, they become irritated by people who appear slower than themselves. This becomes especially true if Objective Thinkers also have the Low Analytical trait (exposed eyelid) as well. With this trait cluster, they quickly see the whole picture without necessarily needing all the details. The challenge for Objective Thinkers lies in the fact that they tend to jump to conclusions before getting all the information. This is often seen in individuals who excel at sports, especially in such activities as snowboarding, downhill skiing, car racing, football, and tennis. This trait offers a plus in any activity, for which quick reaction benefits the person involved.

Objective Thinker

Clyde, a newspaper reporter, who had the Objective Thinking trait, interviewed me when I published my first book *It's All in the Face*. He took about five minutes to get a general overview of face analysis, and he presumed knew all there was to know. The article ended up as a poor representation of my work, leaving me disappointed with the result. Three years later, I produced another book. Despite my efforts to find someone else in the newspaper office to write an article on face reading, Clyde decided it was his job to do the interview. My heart sank.

His opening comment was, "Tell me something about myself." I told him he jumped to conclusions. He said, "You mean I don't get all the details?" I proceeded to give him a personal reading. He wrote the best article I've seen in years.

If you have the Objective Thinking trait, when necessary, take more time to check all the details. This could save you both time and money.

The Objective Thinking trait does serve as a plus where quick decision-making constitutes part of the job, such as if you work as a paramedic, firefighter, or race car driver. People with sloped-back foreheads have much faster responses to situations in the moment.

Famous Faces

Tony Blair, David Letterman, Serena Williams, Katie Couric

Relationships

When Objective Thinkers enter into a relationship with Sequential Thinkers, these opposite traits cause some annoyances. The Objective Thinkers see the Sequential Thinkers as deliberately slow. They will try to hurry their partners up, which then creates more pressure, which can turn into heated arguments.

One man with the Objective Thinker trait thought his wife was being deliberately slow to annoy him. When he discovered after twenty-five years of marriage that his wife was a Sequential Thinker, he admitted he had no idea this was how she processed information.

No matter how short—or long-lived the relationship is, if you have either of these two traits, don't expect everyone to move at your speed. That relieves a lot of aggravation in relationships of all types.

Children

Children with the Objective Thinking trait may get very impatient sometimes when things aren't moving along fast enough for them. They will have a tendency to jump to conclusions without getting all the details.

Sales

Clients with the Objective Thinking trait, sometimes presume they know what you are going to say without first getting all the details. They just want to move things on, and as a result, they may miss a few of the important details. Make sure you review the product or service with them before they leave. This will avoid any misunderstanding about what was said.

Careers

Objective Thinkers enjoy working as firefighters, law enforcement officers, stand-up comedians, salespeople, paramedics, newscasters, taxi drivers, or in any career or sport where quick reactions are needed.

Dwells in the Past or Looks to the Future

Backward Balance
More head behind the ear

Forward Balance
More face in front of the ear

This facial feature represents a time orientation trait. Individuals with this trait base their decisions or thoughts on past experiences or what is happening today or what is going to happen in the future. They look ahead and plan for the future, whereas individuals with Backward Balance focus on the now or yesterday. Whether or not someone has the Forward or Backward Balance trait, it is determined by looking at whether he or she has more head in the front of the ear or behind the ear. If one has more head in front of the ear, this individual thinks in terms of the present and the future and has Forward Balance. If one has more head behind the ear, one thinks in terms of the past which indicates Backward Balance.

Forward Balance

In addition to quantifying time orientation, the Forward Balance trait also measures how much a person needs recognition or appreciation. Everyone needs some degree of recognition; however, when that need becomes significant, individuals with this trait enjoy the limelight. Forward Balance individuals love applause from an audience and sometimes "ham it up" to get attention. This becomes more noticeable if these people also have the Dramatic Appreciation (outer corner of the eyebrow flares upward) trait.

Individuals with the Forward Balance trait love to call attention to themselves, and they will do so with loud behavior, praise for putting on a good show, or by telling jokes. Sometimes, they can be so full of themselves that consideration of other people's feelings does not enter into their thoughts. For this reason, in the extreme form of this trait, Forward Balance individuals can come across as less considerate. For example, a young lady with this trait, Lisa, likes to get attention and would do anything, including making noises or make people laugh, to draw attention to herself. When she teased a

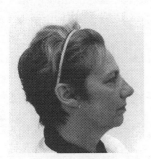

waiter or waitress, her husband would get really annoyed. He was embarrassed by his wife's behavior. She never considered how her banter affected him.

If you have the Forward Balance trait, make sure you take the time to recognize what others have achieved. Don't bring attention to yourself at the cost of others. Learn to take a "backseat" and give those around you the opportunity to be recognized for their contribution or performance.

Forward Balance

Famous Faces
Pierce Brosnan, Tony Blair, Dame Judy Dench

Relationships
If your partner has the Backward Balance trait and he or she constantly brings up past negative situations or remarks, you will find this boring. Plus your Backward Balance partner will feel you are not interested in what he or she has to say, and he or she may feel cut off. Remind your partner that hanging on to negative situations could be holding them back; they need to look at the positive side of life.

Children
Forward Balance children need recognition. Parents must make sure this trait in their children is channeled in the right direction. Don't wait for your children to act out before you praise them; beat them to it, and praise them liberally for what they have done. If Forward Balance children don't get the recognition they need at home, or they are not given tasks or activities that challenge them, they can end up joining gangs or similar peer groups. Get them involved with activities such as theater, sports, gymnastics, ballet or anything where they get attention. This is especially important if they also have the Dramatic Appreciation (the outer corner of the eyebrow flares upward) trait.

Sales

Forward Balance people are more focused on the future. They like to plan ahead. So when they are ready to make a decision, everything must be in place. Remember this if you find yourself with a client with this facial feature.

Careers

This Forward Balance trait often is seen in leaders of countries, groups or organizations. These people are dynamic and set policies faster in the moment because they think in terms of the present and the future. Additionally, this trait is found in performers, teachers, professional athletes, and any profession that puts people "on stage."

Backward Balance

People with Backward Balance have more of the head behind the ear. Backward Balance individuals compare tradition and past experiences to present situations. These individuals tend to hang on to past memories whether positive or negative. One client of mine said having the Backward Balance trait was "like constantly checking in the rear view mirror." Sometimes these people sound like "broken records," telling you over and over again about all the negative aspects of their lives. What was done to them years ago never is forgiven. If we hear their woes once, we hear them a thousand times over. They will re-run past negative conversations to the point that it seems almost obsessive. At times, they find it difficult to turn off their inner chatter.

If you have the Backward Balance trait and catch yourself repeating something in your mind or verbally, redirect your thoughts to things currently going on around you. Better yet, find something more positive to think about.

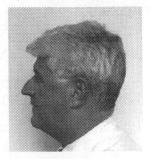

Backward Balance

Backward Balanced people enjoy recognition, but more for what they have achieved or accomplished than for a performance. They feel most comfortable in the background and seldom seek the limelight. They are more interested in their personal activities and how they will accomplish their goals. Thus, they have a tendency to hide their light under a bushel. They need to get the recognition deserved for the accomplishments they achieve, no matter how small.

People with the Backward Balance trait bend over backward to help others. They also are extremely considerate and they often go the extra mile for people. They exhibit this behavior most often.

They enjoy history or anything related to historical interests, such as archeology and genealogy. Combined with the High Acquisitive (cupped-out ears) trait, they enjoy collecting old coins, antiques, or anything of a historical nature. They like visiting old cities as well.

When individuals have a trait combination of Backward Balance, Intense Feelings (long thumb) and Low Tolerance (close-set eyes), this trait cluster indicates that they may have stored bad memories or anger they've held on to for years; any incident or something someone says can trigger their pent-up emotions. If you have this trait cluster and are starting to feel your emotions rushing to the surface, take a walk or a bike ride. Get some exercise to help release your feelings.

When family members have the Backward Balance trait, they tend to be unforgiving of the past. This causes many rifts between parents and children and between siblings.

Holding on to bad memories serves no purpose; let them go. Shift your focus, and fill your life with the good things happening today and the pleasant memories of the past. Heal the wounds, and move on. Focus on what you want to bring into your life.

Often times, people with this trait look good in a more toned red, like the color of wine. When I was giving a talk at a conference, I noticed a woman in the audience was wearing a very old-looking red. I asked her to stand up and explained to the audience how this "old" red, which looked really good on her, probably indicated that she had more of the head behind the ear. After validating this trait in her, the woman then shared that she majored in history at a university. I also mentioned that she would look good in antique jewelry or anything that was more ethnic in design. This would include buying antiques for her home.

When I lived in Stockholm, I loved the simplistic design of the Danish furniture. This represented such a change from the heavy antiques to which I was accustomed in England. The furniture seemed like a whole new world to me. I have found that when individuals wear clear strong reds, which I do, they prefer more contemporary design styles. Over time, I have observed this pattern to be true.

Relationships

If you have this trait, the best thing you can do to have healthy relationships is to let go of negative memories. Your Forward Balance partner and your families will soon be tired of you going on and on about what happened in the past. They no longer want to hear the replayed script, so just tear it up. Forgive and forget.

Children

Jane shared a story with me about a young boy with the Backward Balance trait. He struggled with anxiety about his baseball skill. Every time he went up to pitch, he said a nasty gremlin would tell him he was going to fail and that defeated him. After noticing his badgering baseball gremlin, he actually named him Bert. He would then literally flick him off his shoulder before he went up to the pitching mound, and this made it possible for him to concentrate on his pitching.

This technique can be used in all situations whether it's at exam time or in a situation where the child or adult runs negative situations over and over again in their heads. Or if your children tend to lie in bed and keep running negative situations over and over in their heads, suggest they listen to some music in their head. Or they can imagine themselves playing in the sand or flying a kite. Suggest they think about a topic that will help them relax and take their mind off their concerns.

Sales

Customers with the Backward Balance trait may be hanging on to past situations where things just didn't work out with other companies. Reassure them you will follow through on your promises.

Careers

This trait is often seen in people who choose career as anthropologists, history teachers or contractors who specialize in restoring old buildings.

Indecision: One ear is further back than the other

The Indecision trait is best observed when standing behind a person while they are sitting down in a chair. Look over the top of the head, and notice if one ear appears to be farther forward than the other. If this is really noticeable, this person will come across as being very indecisive.

These individuals will go back and forth when making a decision. You'll think they have made up their minds, and suddenly, it's a different story. Dawn stated that she found making decisions extremely difficult. She would ask all of her friends, or anyone who she met, what should she do rather than decide on her own. Based on their advice, she would then make a decision. She had one ear further back than the other.

If an individual has a lot of asymmetry in the face (Mood Swings), this will exacerbate their decision-making problems. If the person's life is out of balance or they feel stressed, he or she will become unpredictable as well. If you have the Indecision trait, make a decision and stay with it, unless you discover good reason to change your mind.

If you find you really cannot make up your mind, go for a vigorous walk, work out at a gym, or go for a bike ride. This will help clear your head, and you will be in a better state of mind for making a decision.

Relationships

If your partner constantly changes plans at the last minute, you might want to give them a gentle reminder about this tendency, or ask them in a playful voice, "Are you changing your mind again?" Then they won't get so annoyed at you pointing this habit out to them. If you have this trait and find yourself going back and forth on decisions, look at both sides of the decision then make up your mind, and stay with what you've decided to do. Otherwise, your indecisiveness could be annoying to your partner.

Children

If your children have this trait and constantly change their minds about things, find ways to help them stay with their commitments. Otherwise, their friends and family members will find their actions confusing.

Sales

If you find your customers with this trait are constantly changing their minds, you might want to ask them for a firm commitment.

Careers

This trait has no applications for careers.

Competitive

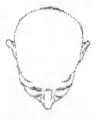 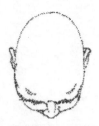

High Competitive
The head is wider at the back
compared with the front

Low Competitive
Head is narrower above the ears
compared with the back

The shape of the head indicates how competitive a person is by nature.

If a person's head is wider above the ear compared with the front of the head, this indicates a naturally competitive personality. Many, if not all, professional sports players, politicians, and chief executive officers of companies, as well as people who work in sales and marketing, have this trait. Their competitiveness drives them to beat their competitors and to move forward on their ideas.

If we were to look down from above at the head of a competitive person, it would appear to be in a wedge shape. Individuals with this wedge-shaped head get an enormous thrill from the enjoyment of winning. For them, competition represents what life is all about, and nothing beats winning.

Low Competitive individuals' heads are wider in the front than the back. They dislike competition and will be turned off by the competitive nature of others, actually scorning people who are competitive.

High Competitive

Competitive individuals are the high achievers of the world. They constantly strive to outdo the other person or compete within themselves to achieve better results. This trait helps them accomplish and produce more results than other people.

Competitive individuals have the desire to win. In the extreme, they often come across as aggressive and may appear hostile to others. They have a great sense of wanting to get ahead at all costs. When High Competitive individuals feel challenged, they tend to fight back out of their desire to win. They need to focus on the pleasure of doing well rather than on winning regardless of the odds or how they win.

Pat was extremely competitive. She liked to exceed her daily goals and complete them early. She put a time on each goal and then competed against the clock. She also liked to compete with her husband to get other people's attention. He had a natural rapport with people, and she wanted people to like her as much as they liked her husband. Others saw her as being pushy. She could not understand why they saw her that way, until she realized that her behavior was so aggressive. It was natural for this petite woman who was a powerhouse—to push ahead. Pat found exercise provided one way to balance this energy; she felt so much better after doing so and the rest of the day unfolded more smoothly.

High Competitive

Bill, another Competitive client of mine, did not like to compete, unless he knew he could win. He wanted to be the best, and he wanted the world to know it.

Another client shared with me that when people blocked her way from doing what she wanted or needed to do, she almost felt emotionally violent. Plus her intolerance skyrocketed. When she wanted to do something, nothing could hold her back. Sometimes people hated her for these traits.

The energy of the High Competitive person can scare people off. When companies look for a "race horse" (jargon for a competitive executive) and get one, they're not always quite sure how to handle that person's energy. When things need to be done at work, the High Competitive person jumps several management levels to get projects accomplished. They find it extremely irritating when people do not take action.

One man I met who had the High Competitive trait really liked to win. He would brag about his success at any opportunity. "Look at me! I won. I'm the best." It really annoyed his friends because he came across as so full of himself.

If you have this trait, learn to be less aggressive when it is not appropriate to express this characteristic. Know when to turn your aggression and competitiveness off. Recognize other people's achievements regardless of whether they came in first or not.

When a difference exists from one side of the head to the other, this indicates that, for the most part, an individual is competitive, but at other times, they drag their feet. Fellow coworkers may find this confusing, since they will never know what to expect of a person with this combination of traits. For example, there were days when John arrived late to work, which reflected his Low Competitive nature, and other times, he came in early, moving full speed ahead, and expecting everyone else to be operating at the same energy level. This created a lot of stress in the office.

On a positive note, we need these highly driven competitive people. They make things happen and move projects forward.

Often times we read in the newspaper about people who despite all odds, have come from extreme poverty, and risen to the top. By nature they strive to move ahead and wonder why others struggle. If individuals are less competitive, they can certainly succeed in life, they just have to be more persistent or hire someone to handle the sales and marketing for them.

Low Competitive

These individuals have no interest in competing. They play a sport for the pleasure and enjoyment of it. Winning is not important. To them, competitiveness actually takes the pleasure out of the activity. They like everyone to have a chance to win.

I met Ann at an event in England. She expressed to me that she absolutely hated competition. She had been seeing a therapist, for a number of months, to help her get over her intense dislike of being around competitive people. Both her sister and her mother were extremely competitive, so this presented a huge issue for Ann. I quickly checked the width of her head, and I explained to Ann that by nature, she was not a Competitive person, and she did not need to be. She looked at me in total astonishment, unable to believe that I could determine this in less than a minute.

I asked Ann to describe what being competitive meant to her. She expressed her anger and resentment at how competition had negatively affected her life and how she felt pressured to compete in many ways. I then asked her to describe what it would be like to be a non-competitive person. The tension left her face; she looked relaxed as she described her natural self. Believing that she could be this person, it removed a load off her shoulders; she no longer felt the need to act in a way that felt foreign and uncomfortable for her.

Ann's goal was to become a professional singer, but the competitive nature of the business turned her off. I confirmed that she had the Low Competitive trait. I suggested she let her agent do the competing for her, leaving her to perfect her singing skills. She left our meeting with such a look of relief on her face.

A Low Competitive woman shared with me that she and her friends had stayed at a cabin at Lake Tahoe for the weekend. In the evening, everyone except herself decided to play bridge. Beth did not like the aggressiveness of the game. All evening long, she could hear them arguing and trying to outdo each other. She found the competitive atmosphere most unpleasant; it put a damper on the weekend. The individuals involved in the game thought it was great fun. For them, it was all about winning, it gave them a high.

Individuals with the Low Competitive trait are not salespeople; they can take on sales jobs, but they won't enjoy the constant pressure. Often times, people fall in love with a product and sign up for a multi-level marketing program. When it comes to selling the product, they find this challenging. After a while, they just give up.

Relationships

This trait also can create relationship challenges, particularly if the woman is competitive and her male partner is more of a procrastinator. The competitive woman sees her partner as having a lot of potential, yet he doesn't seem to go anywhere. Or she asks him to do a chore around the house, and he takes forever to get around to doing it. In the end, the Low Competitive man cannot stand the nagging anymore, or the High Competitive woman leaves because she cannot handle what she calls her partner "not doing anything with his life."

If you are Competitive and your partner is not, keep in mind your competitiveness is yours to use. Don't place your own expectations on others; don't expect them to have the characteristics that go with a Competitive personality. Encourage and support them to take action, but don't keep nagging them.

I met with a young man who said his mother was extremely competitive and forceful by nature. She constantly nagged her husband for not meeting her goals. He often did not meet her expectations, and this became a huge conflict in the family—a conflict that finally ended in divorce. As the young man shared the story with me, tears poured down his face. Had she understood her own traits and those of her husband, much of the unpleasantness could have been avoided.

In a relationship, we need to accept our partners for who they are and realize that our goals and aspirations may not be the same as theirs. Some couples believe the myth that "things will change once we're married." Accept each other for who you are and work on mastering your own traits, rather than pointing the finger at the other person for theirs.

When I was lecturing on a cruise, I took my book into the bookstore and spoke to a young man working there about face analysis. I gave him a quick assessment, and I found him to be extremely Competitive. He said his competitive nature was an issue with his fellow coworkers because he was by far the top salesperson. They were jealous of him, and they felt he stole the limelight. He said he'd promote my book on the cruise; he did a fantastic job. My book sales were higher than any other book they had carried. As I said, High Competitive people make great sales-people—especially if they believe in the product they are selling.

Children

Children who are High Competitive need to have an outlet for their competitive and aggressive energy. Enroll them in a sport or activity that allows them to compete.

One young man I met, who was High Competitive in nature, would only sign up for a sport if he could be the best on his team. When his coach moved him up to an older group, he was no longer the star, so he dropped out. This represents somewhat typical behavior for Competitive children. Parents need to help them channel this energy in a positive direction.

If they also have the Dramatic (swept up eyebrows) trait, they will compete for attention. Remind them to acknowledge fellow students for what they have done, no matter how small the achievement.

Sales

If you are an auctioneer, you will certainly see this competitive trait in the people who participate at an event. If there is a popular item up for sale, individuals with this trait will try to out-bid other contenders. If they also have the High Risk-Taking (ring finger longer than index finger) trait, they could well risk all.

Careers

High Competitive people do well in sales and marketing, and as law enforcement officers, race car drivers, and professional athletes of all kinds. They also excel in any activity where they can channel their competitive energy.

The Procrastinator

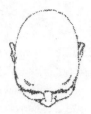

Head narrower at the back compared with the front

Procrastinators (narrow head at the back compared with the front) do not follow through much of the time. They spend too much time thinking about what they are going to do rather than just doing it. They may start something then give up half way through. They think, "Yes, I've always wanted to take that trip or complete that project, and I will one day." Five, ten, twenty years go by and they are still in the dreaming mode.

This trait, despite all other positive traits they have, may be sufficient to deactivate the Procrastinator's potential. Their behavior puzzles many people; people who have this trait seem to have so much potential, yet don't seem to move on with their lives. They talk about their projects and dreams, but unless they schedule them into their daily calendars, they remain a dream.

One young man I met who had the Procrastinator trait, told me he grew up with his parents constantly telling him he was a lazy good-for-nothing individual, and that he would never amount to much. At the time I met him, he and his girl friend were living with his parents. His girlfriend asked me to read his face. After explaining the Procrastination trait to him, to which he definitely related, I asked him what he wanted to change in his life. He said he wanted to move out of his parent's home. Judging by the expression on his girlfriend's face, she definitely liked that idea. As it turned out, he'd been talking about moving out for some time, but he hadn't done it. With just a short coaching session, he announced his intention to move out within the next four weeks. The next day, he sought me out to share his plan of action and to tell me he had already informed his parents of the upcoming move. For him, taking a step toward his goal took a big weight off his shoulders. (Yes, he did follow through.)

Some of you may ask, "Why didn't he just move out?" It's hard for people with this trait to move forward on their ideas. It's like having a ball and chain around their ankles. Enthusiasm for taking action exists within them, but they almost feel overwhelmed by the idea of moving their ideas forward. For instance, a lawyer with this trait said he worked in litigation, which meant there were deadlines to meet each day. If he didn't have deadlines, he said, it would probably take him forever to complete anything. The deadlines gave him a reason to keep moving forward.

Many people who attend motivational workshops get really inspired to move their goals forward. These programs should include methods that teach participants how to take their ideas and make them into reality. Or they should offer the Procrastinators continued support to help them take their goals to the next level or take action steps to actually reach them.

The solution for Procrastinators comes in using short lists, such as three things on a to-do list and deadlines for getting those things done. Long lists do not work for these individuals nor do long-term goals, unless they create deadlines. They need a plan for one week out not one month out. Once this methodology is put into practice, people with this trait find it easier to move forward on their ideas and projects.

Procrastinators will need to work at this throughout their lives, though. The desire to wait, rather than to take action, doesn't just go away. The more these individuals become aware that they put things off, the greater the chances are of them completing their projects on time.

Relationships

Again, this trait creates challenges in relationships, especially if the man is the Procrastinator. Let's say the Procrastinator's wife asks him to do something, and several days, weeks, or even months go by and still the project has not been done. This annoys the wife to the point that her partner feels she is nagging him to get it done. To solve the problem, the two people either could agree upon what needs to be done that day or write a short to-do list and see how that works. (Remember to keep the list brief.) Sometimes, the other partner just has to take on the Procrastinator's responsibility, especially when planning a trip; the Procrastinator just may not do it, and the other partner must know that is the case.

Children

Give deadlines to children who have this trait, especially where homework is concerned. If you have asked them to tidy up their room, for instance, give them a time by when you want that completed.

Don't label children who have the Procrastinator trait as lazy. If they have the motivation, they will go for the things they are passionate about.

Sales

The Procrastinator could show up as a client who never gets back to you or who doesn't follow through on their commitments. As a salesperson, get the Procrastinator to give you a time frame with which you can both work.

Careers

There are no applications for this trait. However, if you have the Procrastination Trait and you are thinking of changing careers, create a short-term plan of action. Write a short list of what needs to be done each day in order to move your life forward.

Chapter Eight

The Jaw

Authoritative
Square Jaw
Likes to be in charge

The wider the jaw, the more authoritative a person sounds and appears, which explains why this trait is called Authoritative. Hillary Clinton, Sarah Palin, and David Letterman are good examples of people with this feature. They also have wide faces (High Self-Confidence) that adds to their authoritative appearance. A narrow jaw line looks less authoritative, such as the British Prime Minister David Cameron. He certainly appears less authoritative than Tony Blair or Edward Kennedy. He does not carry such an authoritative air as a leader who has a wider jaw.

The wide jaw gives resonance to the voice. Individuals with this trait come across as strong and more assertive. These Authoritative individuals have a natural tendency to take charge. They find it hard to take a backseat, especially when others hesitate. When they see other people fumbling or showing hesitation, from their perspective, these individuals are not trying. At times, Authoritative people come across as opinionated.

When High Authoritative individuals step into a room, they do not have to say a word. They have a strong presence, and they look as if they are in control of the situation. This air of authority is heightened if the person also has the High Self-Confidence (wide face) trait. These individuals can seem quite intimidating, which provides a distinct asset, at times, when strong leadership is needed. They command respect, like to be in charge, and are decisive in the way they speak. The minute these individuals feel threatened, their voices become louder, particularly if they have coarse hair (Less Sensitive). For this reason, High Authoritative individuals need to cultivate a warmer tone in their voice.

Women who have this trait should avoid using strong colors, such as navy, black, royal blue, and bright red, when in a general meeting with their business associates or department. Cheryl was the head of her department, and she comes across as being extremely authoritative. She often would wear strong colors when attending a meeting. Her fellow employees found her very intimidating and remained silent in the meeting, rather than express their concerns. Once she received the advice to wear softer colors, everyone relaxed and a lot more was accomplished in her meetings. Fellow employees did not feel as threatened.

Authoritative

When working with people who have the Authoritative trait, do not accept their apparent take-charge attitude when they actually are not in charge. Understand that this can be their style of expression and their natural way of communicating.

If you have this trait, think about how you may sound to others who have a less authoritative nature. Develop an awareness of how you communicate with them, soften your voice, and try not to be too pushy. Think of a way to change your approach so it produces a more positive outcome.

You can use this trait to your advantage when needed, but be prepared to back off when appropriate. If you come across as being too authoritative or aggressive, it will put people off. This could create hostility, and it could work against you when you need support from others.

Famous Faces
Hilary Clinton, Sarah Palin, Edward Kennedy, Tom Cruise

Relationships
A High Authoritative person who comes across as being too aggressive in relationships may smother their less authoritative partner's growth. Let the other person have their say too.

Children
If your children are aggressive, it might be a good idea to remind them how this works against them. Teach them how to use the High Authoritative trait in a positive way.

Sales

If your customer comes across as being High Authoritative and demanding, find ways to calm them down. They don't have to have the last word.

Careers

No specific careers exist for people who have the Authoritative trait. Whatever job you choose, just make sure you don't come across as being too authoritative with your fellow coworkers. Be there to support them.

Low Authoritative

People with narrow jaws tend to be less assertive and do not come across as being so Authoritative. However, the addition of other traits will make them appear more assertive, such as the Administrative nose (likes to be in charge). If they are very competitive, this will strengthen their style of communication. If they also have exposed eyelids (bottom line) this trait cluster is more "in-your-face," pushy, and assertive.

If you have a narrow jawline (Low Authoritative) and fine hair (Sensitive), cultivate a stronger and more decisive tone, especially when interacting with people who have wider faces and jaws. Be gently assertive to individuals exhibiting authoritative behavior; let them know you intend to be in charge, and you want to be heard.

Also, if you are a Low Authoritative person, wear deeper neutral colors, such as navy, black, forest green, burgundy, or dark purple. These more formal colors along with a light colored shirt or blouse, will support your verbal and visual message. It will bring up the energy seen in the face. This is very important when going for an interview or giving a presentation; darker colors will give you an air of confidence.

Famous Faces
George Bush, Prince William, whereas, Prince Harry has the wider jaw and comes across as being more assertive.

Relationships
If you are less assertive, make sure you let your partner know what your feelings are about decisions that are made. Otherwise, he or she may just take over and not take your preferences into consideration.

Low Authoritative

Children
This trait is not fully developed in children, until they are in their teenage years. The behavior may be seen in the earlier years as children being less assertive or shy. This is a term which is often used by parents which may reinforce their behavior.

Sales

Low Authoritative clients will be easier people to work with. They won't come across as being pushy. If they have the Administrative nose (likes to be in charge) and are High Competitive (head wider at the back), they could come across as being more "in-your-face," especially if they have the exposed eyelid (Bottom Line).

Careers

This trait is seen in all careers.

Automatic Resistance

Pointed Chin
Very stubborn

People with wedge-shaped jaws, or who have a pointed chin, come across as stubborn, and they do not like being told what to do. They put up a strong resistance and automatically say, "No," when they feel any hint of pressure. The more they are pushed, the more they dig in their heels and refuse to budge. Working with people with this trait, which is called Automatic Resistance or stubborn, makes you feel like you're pushing against a brick wall. However, despite their stubbornness, they can be easily persuaded if you provide them with reasons why you need them to do something. An explanation works far better than pressure with these individuals.

When Karen, who has the stubborn feature or Automatic Resistance trait, is told what to do, she appears to be cooperating on the outside, but inside, she is rebelling. Push her too far and the flag will go up, indicating a very strong "No." Just when everything appears to be okay, the Automatic Resistance individual explodes. Karen found that when she felt stressed at work, walking, yoga, and tai chi helped balance her day. Without these activities, she said, she would become an emotional wreck. They helped her relax, and she felt less stressed.

On the outside, Automatic Resistance individuals appear to handle pressure much better than most. However, they keep things bottled up inside while seemingly handling a situation.

If you have this trait, rather than automatically saying "No" to everything, try saying "Let me get back to you on that." or, "I'll think it over." This avoids much of the frustration experienced by other people you encounter, and it keeps communication open. Additionally, ask yourself what you gain by being so stubborn and rejecting ideas, situations, etc., without justification. What are you really resisting? Are you being reasonable, and is your resistance based on principles or feelings? If you find yourself reacting when someone tells you what to do, try not to get so uptight. Do something to relieve the tension, such as going for a walk, listening to a piece of music, or engage in any activity that helps you relax.

When working with individuals who have the Automatic Resistance trait, try asking them to do something rather than telling them to do so. You'll find they are more willing to cooperate with you if you use that approach. Ask them what can be done to speed up the process. Get them involved with decisions, rather than telling them what you have decided; the former approach keeps options open, while the latter doesn't allow any options.

Automatic Resistance

Famous Faces
Katie Couric, Sarah Palin, David Letterman, Vladimir Putin

Relationships
If your partner has the Automatic Resistance trait, try asking, rather than telling him or her to do something. Otherwise, he or she will come across as being extremely stubborn and less willing to cooperate with you. If you have the stubborn trait, try to be more flexible.

Children
When stubbornness is a problem in young children, explain the reasons you want them to do something, rather than saying "You have to, that's why." When possible, involve them in the decision; then they will not be quite as stubborn. When you give children and adults motivating reasons to do what you ask, they will come around.

Sales
Don't push clients with the Automatic Resistance trait into purchasing your product or service; persuade them with the reasons they should do so.

Pugnacity

Square Chin
The love of debate

Pugnacity is determined by the square-ness of the chin. Good examples of people with this trait include David Letterman, John Major, and tennis player Roger Federer; they all have square chins. Individuals with this trait love to get into good meaty discussions. They fight for what they believe in, whether it is a favorite cause or social justice. These individuals never give up; they have a "fighting spirit." They do well in debate or mediation because they are good at presenting both sides of a situation to their clients.

The Pugnacity trait indicates the ability for an individual with this trait, to physically and verbally respond to situations in the moment. A square-chinned friend and I visited a local court session in England. After listening to several cases, we decided to leave. As we exited the courtroom, a policewoman followed us out, and she asked what we had been doing in court. My Pugnacious companion lashed out at her, explaining in no uncertain terms that we had every right as English citizens to attend court sessions. It was a much stronger and more confrontational response than necessary or appropriate. I spoke to my friend afterward, and over time, he has learned to gain control over this automatic response. Modifying behavioral tendencies that arise from traits does not happen overnight, though. It takes a strong consistent desire to change the behavior.

Individuals with the Pugnacity trait will outwardly "appear" to be going along with a situation or a decision. However, they may not feel that way, or agree, on the inside. Later, they may well pull out of their commitment because the project or situation did not work out as they hoped.

If a person has the Pugnacity and the Construction (Square head) traits, this adds to one's inability to remain committed. One gets involved with good intentions of following through, only to realize, once again, they don't want to continue with the activity. This can prove confusing to people whom they work with, who probably thinks all is well up until the moment the Pugnacious coworker backs out.

If you have this trait, let other people whom you work with know your expectations up front, rather than just going along with the situation to see how it pans out. Suggest that you review developments in a month to see if the project or situation remains something to which you are willing to commit.

A look at Maria's face clearly showed her square chin, a facial feature that belied her pugnacious nature. Maria was always ready to jump in with her opinion, whether it was solicited or not. She liked to get involved in discussions and say what was on her mind. She enjoyed setting a story and facts right. Growing up with six brothers, however, her interest in expressing her opinions had been put on the back burner. Now as an adult, she thrived on getting together with friends and having a good debate. She told me that she and her friends had agreed not to agree. In her work, she helped couples resolve conflicts, work she really enjoyed.

Pugnacity

Sometimes people with the Pugnacity trait go out of their way to pick a verbal, not a physical, fight. If you have this trait, keep in mind that lashing out at someone does not provide a solution. Ask yourself, how would you feel if someone lashed out at you?

If people with this trait also have the Intense Feelings (long thumb) trait, they should be aware of the importance of mastering this trait combination. In a situation that makes them want to enter into a verbal assault, they should think of another way to handle the situation that isn't so aggressive. If you find yourself with someone who has this aggressive behavior, suggest in a quiet tone that he or she talk about the situation before responding, so things don't get out of hand.

Many people with the Pugnacity trait say they find exercise of any sort, in particular running, boxing, or working out at a gym, or engaging in any activity that gave them a physical outlet helped to channel this energy enormously. The French actor Gérard Depardieu once stated in an interview that if he had not taken up acting, he might have ended up in prison. He has a very square chin.

I have often noticed that people with square chins love to kayak. I was at a meeting one day, and I noticed a man standing at the back of the room who had the Pugnacity trait. I suggested he might like to go kayaking. He had just mentioned to his wife that day that he wanted to buy a kayak.

Famous Faces

Bill Gates, Deepak Chopra, Nelson Mandela, Martha Stewart, some of your top rugby players have this trait

Relationships

A partner who has the Pugnacious trait may come across as argumentative. When frustrated, he or she may even lash out at their partner. If you have this trait and you feel this energy coming to the surface, go out and exercise. This will help channel the energy positively and diffuse it.

Children

In children, the Pugnacity trait may be easier to observe in their behavior than in their facial features. This trait is not developed until they are in their teenage years. If one of the parents has this trait, then the chances are the child will inherit similar behavior. This becomes evident once they have passed puberty. If your child has pugnacious tendencies, enroll them in sports or in any activity where they can channel their energy.

Sales

A customer with this trait might appear argumentative. However, know that they just want to get to the meat of the discussion and debate it with you.

Careers

People with the Pugnacity trait make good trial lawyers, mediators, rugby players, boxers, and male gymnasts. They may even enjoy working for an environmental or humanitarian cause.

Tenacity

Protruding Chin
Very tenacious

The Tenacity trait is indicated by the amount of chin protruding forward when viewed from the side. The more the chin protrudes forward, the more tenacious the person becomes. Jay Leno provides a great example of a High Tenacious person. A receding chin indicates the Low Tenacious trait. A High Tenacious person sticks with things until completion, while a Low Tenacious person tends to let go of situations too quickly.

Once Tenacious individuals get their teeth into a project or relationship, they hang on 'til the bitter end. They have a tendency to stick with whatever they are doing, right or wrong, good or bad. They can take their commitment to a relationship, job, or anything else to extreme levels, even when doing so might be against their best interests. They need to realize when it's time to let go, rather than staying and hoping things will work out.

If you have the Tenacious trait, hang on for the right reasons, but do not continue to keep "hanging on" when your cause seems lost. Before starting a new project or venture, set reasonable goals. Define what you really want to happen before tackling a problem. Then as time goes on, you will know whether or not to hang on and why. Learn to let go if what you are doing does not work or fit into your long-term plans.

Tenacity

Low Tenacious people (receding chin) do not "hang on for the sake of hanging on." They are more willing to let go of situations and projects when they are no longer useful. This makes these people easier to work with. However, under pressure, they may well walk off the job. They don't have the "stick-to-it-ness" necessary for hard times.

People who lack tenacity may end relationships too soon. If you have this trait, ask yourself whether you are letting go too soon. What might happen if you hung in just a little longer? Set goals; this will help you get through the times when you just want to give up. Goals remind you why you are taking the task on, and it gives you something which to focus upon. When you feel ready to back off, stop and review your goals. If you are still going in the right direction, you might want to hang in there for a while longer before giving up or getting out.

Famous Faces
Bill Gates, Anthony Hopkins, Jennifer Aniston, Judy Dench

Relationships
If either partner has the High Tenacious trait, they will make the extra effort to make the relationship work should challenges come up. They won't give up to easily. If one partner has the Low Tenacious trait, however, he or she may give up on the relationship without trying hard to make it work or to walk out when times get tough.

Children
Children with the High Tenacious trait are determined, and they will not give up too quickly once they have set their minds on something. It adds to their ability to follow through on their commitment. Add the Competitive trait, now you have a very determined child or teenager.

Sales
This trait has no applications in the area of sales.

Careers
This trait is seen in all careers.

Physical Motive

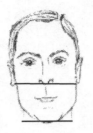

Length of this area of the face compared with the entire length of the face

Restless

The need to be on the go
Distance from base of nose to chin

The Physical Motive trait is determined by measuring the length of the face from the base of the chin to the base of the nose. This measurement is compared with the entire length of the face. A special tool was designed to get an accurate measurement. The longer is the space between the chin and the nose, the more restless the person's nature is. Individuals with this trait are constantly on the go. They like to be physically active and doing something at all times.

In contrast, the shorter the space between the chin and the nose, the more the person uses their mind. They respond to situations by sorting things out mentally, rather than physically responding to them. The Physical Motive person leaps to action, while the person with the opposite trait sits and thinks about it.

Physical Motive individuals have an enormous amount of stamina and a seemingly endless supply of energy. They keep going when others give up. Individuals with this trait have to be constantly in motion. Just sitting and watching television, for instance, is quite challenging to them, particularly if they also have short legs. (People with short legs tend to be restless.) These individuals find it hard to relax. Part of them wants to get up and do something more constructive.

One woman expressed her frustration over the fact that her husband was constantly on the go. He never seemed to take the time to sit with her in the evenings. Her father-in-law behaved in the same way. This constituted to be one of her biggest complaints. She showed me a photo of both of them. They both had the long lower face feature for the Physical Motive trait, and she confirmed that they both had short legs as well.

The next time you watch a soccer, rugby, or football game, notice how many of the players have short to medium legs (built to be on their feet) and long lower faces

(High Physical Motive). Many boxers and wrestlers have this trait, along with square chins (Pugnacity) as well.

Mark, who had short legs and the Restless trait, worked a desk job. He complained that he lived a large portion of his life feeling like an animal in a cage. Working out at a gym gave him an outlet for his frustrations; it released him from his boredom and gave him more energy. This greatly improved his relationship with his family because he stopped taking his frustrations out on them.

Sally had a trait combination of High Tolerance (wide-set eyes) and Physical motive. She found it extremely difficult to focus during her early years in school, and she had a hard time sitting still for long periods of time. She continued to struggle with that later in life as well. When she exercised, however, the problem went away; the exercise brought balance to her day.

Physical Motive

I happen to have the High Physical Motive trait. My husband tells me I need to hike a mountain each day—maybe two mountains. To survive sitting still on long airline flights, I get up extra early the day of my trip and go for a brisk walk. I never take the moving walkways or escalators at the airport. Walking through the terminals gives me some added exercise before boarding the plane. If you have this trait, make sure you get up during the flight, move around, and stretch your legs.

If you find yourself getting irritable or restless during the day, take time out and go for a brisk walk. Your mind will feel clearer, and you'll be able to focus better on your work. You're productivity will increase as well. This is really important if you are writing a book or term paper or working on your accounts. By exercising and taking a short break, you help avoid the irritation of sitting, you will retain focus and accomplish more.

Famous Faces
Simon Cowell, Bill Clinton, Andre Agassi, Lindsey Davenport

Relationships
People who score high on the Physical Motive trait like to be where the action is happening as well as to be physically active. They find it hard to slow down and relax. They have so much energy that sometimes, they do not know what to do with themselves. If their partners have the opposite trait, they may find it difficult to keep

up. Plus the High Physical Motive partner may get frustrated with their less physically inclined partner—and vice versa. Find activities you can both enjoy.

Children

Children who have the Physical Motive trait have boundless energy. This energy needs to be channeled into activities such as soccer, tennis, dancing, gymnastics, or any athletic activity.

On Halloween, the children in my neighborhood were knocking on my door and calling out, "Trick or Treat." Upon hearing that I was English, one young man started to sing, "I am a Londoner, yes, I am." In return, I asked if he would like me to read his face, and I proceeded to do so. I told him he would be good at sports, whereupon he asked which sport. "Soccer," I replied. He was totally amazed by my accuracy. The young man had the trait combination of High Physical Motive (long lower face), plus short legs (built to be on their feet), Objective Thinking (sloped forehead), and High Competitive (head wider at the back compared with the front).

His friends then all requested a reading. As they turned around to walk down the path, they shouted out to their parents, "You'll never believe what this lady just told us." They definitely remembered that Halloween.

When the trait cluster of short legs, Physical Motive, High Tolerance (wide-set eyes), and High Competitive (head wider at the back compared with the front) is found in children or teenagers, they find sitting at desks a challenge. Add the Construction (square forehead) trait, these children will be quickly bored by repetition, and you can see how students quickly are labeled as having Attention Deficit Disorder (ADD). Some do have ADD; however, I think this label is overly used today by many well-intended coaches and therapists. Now that many schools have cut sports programs, this will add to the number of students having a hard time sitting still and focusing on their school work. They need an outlet for this energy every day.

If your children's school has cut back on its sports programs, enroll your Physical Motive child in after school sports. If this is not an option, find a group of parents who would like to organize some after school games for the children. They will be more settled in the evening and do better in school.

Sales

This trait has no specific applications in sales.

Careers

The High Physical motive trait has no specific application in the area of careers. However, if you have this trait and have trouble sitting at a desk for long periods of time, make sure you include exercise in your schedule on a regular basis.

Mental Motive

Short space compared
with the length of the face

Stimulated by Mental Activity
Short space between base of chin and nose

People who have a shorter distance from the base of the chin to the base of the nose have the Mental Motive trait. They are stimulated by mental challenges. Mental activity is as consuming to them, as physical activity is to those with the Physical Motive trait. People who have the Mental Motive trait accomplish more through the mental process than through physical action. Also, without a mental challenge, they may become bored in their jobs.

If these short-lower-faced people also are long-legged, a physical feature that lends itself to being off their feet, these individuals find it easy to spend hours sitting and reading a book, watching a video or television, or simply just sitting and thinking about life in general. To others, they appear to be "couch potatoes." However, they also enjoy spending time playing chess, bridge, or any activity that requires a lot of thought.

Individuals with this trait need to make sure they include some physical activity scheduled on a regular basis, such as working out at a gym, bicycling, playing golf, or swimming. Just as the High Physical Motive person needs to take time out for mental activity, the High Mental Motive person needs to take time out for exercise.

High Mental Motive individuals spend a lot of time in their heads with their thoughts. They think things through, and they can entertain themselves for hours in their heads. This can be as exhausting as any physical activity. They need to get out of their heads and have more fun. Jennifer, a client of mine with a short lower face, found her mental activity satisfying. She felt happy keeping herself company for hours, and she enjoyed the thinking process. At times, however, thinking so much worked against her; she would become obsessive about what was not working in her life. A fine line exists between a contemplative thought and obsessing over about a particular subject or idea. Using meditation, she was able to work through her obsessive thoughts.

If you have the High Mental Motive trait, make sure you balance your mental activity with physical needs. Take up yoga to balance your energy.

Famous Faces
Vladimir Putin, Steven Spielberg, Madeline Albright

Relationships
This trait has no real relationship applications. If you or your partner has the High Mental Motive trait, you may need to stop spending so much time in your head working out issues. Come down to earth now and again, and share your thoughts with your partner.

Mental Motive

Children
Children who have this trait need intellectual stimulation to keep them interested in school or activities.

Sales
If your client has the High Mental Motive trait, they will give the product or service they are considering a lot more thought. They'll run the idea through their head, until they are completely satisfied they are making the right decision.

Careers
This trait can be seen in all careers. If professional sports players have the High Mental Motive trait, they play a mental game rather than a physical game.

CHAPTER NINE

THE FOREHEAD

Imagination

Mounds
Mounds just below the hairline

Imagination is indicated by the raised mounds formed on the left and right side of the forehead, located just below the hairline. The more pronounced these mounds, the greater a person's imagination.

The word "imagination" conveys the power to visualize freely without getting too far-fetched into fantasies. In other words, imagination allows a person to be specific in their visualizations. An individual with the High Imagination trait can form mental images or concepts easily.

I recently met a young man who was working as a parking garage attendant. Noticing he had all the facial features that indicated he was creative, including the Imagination, raised mounds on his forehead, I asked him if he was attending college. He said he wasn't, and he explained that he had dropped out of high school. I asked him about his career plans. "Who would want a high school drop out?" he responded.

I then shared with him what I do, and I told him that I could see he was an extremely creative individual. I suggested he try his hand at writing, editing text or films. His said, "Oh, I am always noticing the mistakes made in films and wondering why they miss them. I often thought I could do a better job."

I suggested that he should take a class on film editing. He took my hands and said, "This morning, I was really feeling in at the lowest point in my life, you have just turned my day around." Hopefully, my suggestions made a difference in his life as well.

When you notice the protruding mounds on someone's forehead just below the hairline, like I did on this young man, these indicate High Imagination and the ability to produce many original ideas. When these mounds are really bulbous, these individuals love to put the whimsy in their work, such as in cartooning. You can see this in their writing, painting, photography, or other creative endeavors as well.

High Imagination also can create strong negative images. Julie, the mother of a young infant, panicked when she wondered what would happen to her baby if she was to faint or pass out. She kept imagining her baby crawling to the toilet, falling in, and drowning. The strength of this mental image caused her to sign up for a first aid class, so she could cope with emergencies. This example shows how sometimes Julie's imagination would take her to extremes—similar to creating a horror movie in her mind. She would get so caught up in the imaginary situation that it almost seemed real to her.

If you have this trait, try not to let your imagination get you carried away into negative images. If and when it does, immediately turn your thoughts to more positive situations and outcomes.

Famous Faces
Tom Hanks, Oprah Winfrey, J. K. Rowing

Relationships
Support your partner in exploring their innate talents. Encourage them to take classes in their creative area of interest.

Children
This trait is not fully developed in children until they are teenagers. However, one can observe their talent when they engage in any creative activity, such as arts and crafts.

Sales
If you notice the Imaginative trait in your client, you might want to ask them if they enjoy art or any other creative activity. This helps you connect with them on a more personal level.

Careers
If, in addition to the raised mounds, the forehead curves out like the sphere of a football (Originality of Ideas), this indicates people with a natural gift for coming up

with creative ideas. I often see these two traits in cartoonists. Coupled with Critical Perception, this trait cluster is often seen in television cameramen.

The Imagination trait is observed in both men and women who are extremely artistic, although it may not manifest as an artistic talent, meaning someone who creates fine art. Instead, you might find these people working as fashion designers, Web designers, make-up artists, or in any career that offers a creative outlet. This trait is often observed in writers or film directors, also photographers.

Interested in People, Information, or Things

Flat forehead   Rounded forehead

Flat forehead: Interested in things

Slightly rounded forehead: Interested in information

Rounded forehead: Interested in people

Individuals with a flat forehead are primarily interested in things and information. If their forehead dips slightly inward, they are more interested in talking about their latest project or whatever they are working on at the moment. This trait is referred to as being Interested in Things as opposed to being Interested in People. If they have the Hermit Line, which is a short line seen on the hand, they enjoy working alone.

Things Focused

When the forehead is slightly concave, one that dips in, these individuals enjoy working with things and information. If they also have the Construction (square forehead) trait, they are less likely to join groups that involve interaction with many people or going to regular meetings. It is not a comfortable situation for them, unless the meeting has a purpose, such as learning about new products or technology or attending an interesting presentation.

At times, people with the Interested in Things trait feel lonely at events, partly because they find it difficult to continue participating in what seems to them a less interesting conversation. They would rather stay home than face what they consider idle chitchat, which they find boring after a while. However, if they meet up with someone who provides more stimulating and interesting conversation, it makes their evening.

If you have the Interest in Things trait, think of ways you can make networking events work for you. Have a plan to get the most out of the event. For instance, engage people in a conversation with you, and discover their interests. You never know where this might lead.

If you meet someone who has this trait, and they also have thin lips (Concise), engage them in the conversation. Once they open up, you'll find them interesting. Individuals with this trait cluster have a knack for handling and processing data. All their activities are made more vital as they learn and understand the facts behind what they do.

If the Interest in Things trait is combined with Construction (square forehead) and Acquisitiveness (cupped out ears), you'll discover these individuals love to collect books and attend workshops or seminars. This trait is often seen in engineers or any career where instruction or the conveying of information is the main activity. I worked with a start-up company helping them place their employees in the right position. One woman with the above traits was so relieved when I suggested she work at the computer. They had placed her in sales, which was a job she did not want to do. Several years later, they shared with me that my suggestions made a significant difference to the success of their company.

If you have the Interested in Things trait, be aware when you may be going on too much about what you do. When attending social events, find out what other people do first before you speak about your interests; give them a chance to share with you what is going on in their life. This will help you build both business and personal relationships.

Relationships

If you are Interested in Things and your partner is Interested in People, and therefore, more social, make an effort to enjoy going to events with him or her. Otherwise, you'll put a damper on many evenings. If you have friends over for dinner, make sure you engage in a conversation that includes everyone, or it may be possible that your other guests will feel left out. Sometimes, the Interested in Things person gets so caught up in their conversation with the person with whom they are talking, they inadvertently neglect others sitting near them.

Children

Sometimes, children with this trait come across as being quiet and may not have many friends at school. Parents should find ways or set up activities to help them be more interactive with their friends or with other children, then they won't feel so left out. Sign them up for classes that provide opportunities for interaction with others their age, such as art, music, sports, or any activity that involves a group of children.

Sales

When making sales presentations to people with this trait, don't waste these individuals' time with unnecessary discussion. Keep your conversation interesting, otherwise they will feel their time is being wasted.

Careers

This trait can be seen in all careers.

Information Focused

People with a flat or slightly round forehead, which is known as an Information person or the Interested in Information trait, will be more social and enjoy sharing information with others.

This trait is often observed in teachers, writers, engineers, or any career where instruction or the conveying of information constitutes the main activity.

People Focused

A rounded forehead that looks like a sphere of a ball when seen from the side profile indicates individuals who enjoy being with people. They are very social. Add full lips (Verbose) to this scenario, and now you have someone who loves to talk. People who have the Interested in People trait are gregarious individuals who enjoy being with people who interest and stimulate them. They love to network and to attend social events on a regular basis.

Famous People

Rounded Forehead: Katie Couric
Flat Forehead: Bill Gates

Relationships

If you have the Interested in People trait, and your partner is more of an Interested in Things person and doesn't like to socialize as much as you do, arrange some activities you both enjoy. Make sure your partner meets up with someone with whom he or she might relate to or have something in common. This will help to break the ice for them and enjoy their evening.

Children

Children who have the Interested in People trait come across as extremely friendly and have a great social life. Encourage them to talk to other children who don't have many friends.

Sales

Clients who are more people focused are easier to work with. They come across as friendly and as more outgoing than the person with the Interested in Things trait.

Careers

People-focused individuals work well in people-oriented careers, such as human resources, nursing, medicine, teaching, customer service, sales, or any occupation where the main focus revolves around interaction with others.

High Impatience/High Concentration

High Impatience
Forehead slopes inward

High Concentration
Forehead slopes outward

These two traits, Impatience and Concentration, are determined from the same area on the head. If the forehead has an inward slope just outside the outer edge of the eyebrow, like one side of an A-frame tent or house, this indicates a person with an impatient personality. If the forehead slopes outward, this person will have the ability to concentrate, or the ability to keep his or her mind on a line of thought and follow it through. This is often seen in people who enjoy research.

Impatience differs from Low Tolerance (close-set eyes). Low Tolerance individuals only put up with something on a short-term basis; Impatience constitutes an irritation that occurs in the very moment something happens. Typically, when an Impatient individual has to wait in line, or people do something that annoys them, they instantly feel an irritation throughout their entire being.

Individuals with High Concentration have a long attention span, whether they are thinking, observing, or doing. A young child with this trait can amaze adults by how long and intently they engage in an activity with complete absorption

High Impatience
People who have the High Impatience trait have minds inclined to move rapidly from one thing to another. They welcome interruptions, especially if they also have the High Tolerance (wide-set eyes) trait, just to take a break from what they are doing. If you struggle to stay focused when studying, for instance, try giving yourself a break every few hours, or less, if needed. This gives you the time to think about something else for a little while without the nagging thought, "I have to stick with what I'm doing." This helps to balance your day, and you'll get far more accomplished. You will approach projects with a fresh mind and determination each time you start again.

High Impatient people are more impatient with others than with themselves. They know the reasons they haven't finished certain projects, but not understanding why someone else is late causes them quite a bit of dismay. They will sit impatiently in the car waiting for other passengers to put in their appearance; their lateness seems intolerable to them. Anything that delays taking action causes them irritation.

Impatient individuals prove valuable in situations where time is at a premium. For example, these people make super airport employees, moving baggage quickly to get it on planes on time, or personal secretaries, swiftly getting messages through.

The disadvantage to this trait, however, lies in the fact that these individuals make others unhappy by nagging them to speed up. In extreme situations, they have even been known to take things out of the other people's hands to speed up results.

High Impatience

Highly Impatient people, who also have the Low Tolerance (close-set eyes) trait, get irritated at things not happening fast enough to suit them. You can see this in aggravated car drivers waiting in rush hour traffic—typical behavior of New York taxi drivers (or those of any other big city).

If you have an Impatient personality and find yourself getting irritated, take a break. Realize other people find your behavior—snatching things away from them or trying to jump to the front of a line—annoying. When you feel particularly impatient, walk around the block or do something different. A new activity will help refresh you.

Famous Faces
Jennifer Aniston, Katie Couric, Anthony Hopkins, Dick Cheney

Relationships
If you find yourself snapping at your partner, just take a break and calm down. Apologize for being so impatient with them.

Children
If your child has this trait and is getting impatient with their homework or with waiting around for a friend or family member, help them find ways to relax. Explain that being impatient doesn't necessarily speed things up.

Sales

If your customer tends to be impatient, speed up the process. If you can't do that, you might say, "We need to go over a number of details, so bear with me for a while."

Careers

This trait can be seen in all careers.

High Concentration

An individual with the High Concentration trait can take a line of thought and carry through the thinking necessary for the entire project from beginning to end. At times, High Concentration individuals start thinking about something they have seen or read and may appear to be a thousand miles away. Often, when they sit down to read a book or newspaper, they become so absorbed they may be oblivious to everyone and everything around them.

High Concentration

A High Concentration husband absorbed in his hobby failed to smell dinner burning. When his wife returned from an errand, she got out of her car and noted smoke pouring out of the kitchen window. She immediately rushed in to find the charcoal remains of the meal.

When this trait is combined with High Analytical (eyelids hidden) and close-set eyes, these are the born researchers. They are mentally patient and capable of carrying out jobs that may be laborious to others. They enjoy spending hours trying to fix problems.

In social situations, people with this trait need to make sure they pay attention to what goes on around them. If High Concentration and Low Tolerance (close-set eyes) are paired, individuals get buried in their own thoughts or any activity in which they engage. If you want to interrupt them, just quietly say, "I need you in a moment," or just lay a hand on their shoulder to get their attention.

Famous Faces
Jon Gosselin, Leonardo DiCaprio

Relationships
If your partner gets caught up in a project for several hours, try not to interrupt them. Or if you are the High Concentration partner, and you need some time to complete something without interruptions, just let your partner know. Otherwise, your partner will feel annoyed by the constant interruptions while working on a lengthy project.

Children

When children with the High Concentration trait work on a project, try not to interrupt them. If you must, give them a five-minute warning before making them stop what they are doing. This gives them time to break away from their activity.

Sales

This trait has no applications for sales.

Careers

This trait can be seen in people working in all types of careers. The High Concentration trait is useful for people who work on long-term projects or conduct research.

CHAPTER TEN

THE CHEEKBONES

Adventurous

Prominent Cheekbones
The love of adventure

The Adventurous trait correlates with how much the cheekbones protrude from the sides and front of the face. Individuals with prominent cheekbones love adventure and need constant change in their daily lives. They want to be where things are happening. They get excited about new experiences and exploring new territories. Adventurous individuals enjoy variety in their day. In repetitive situations, they quickly become bored. People with this trait love to travel, and they often become discoverers and explorers. They also are eager to make changes.

Susan, a woman who had the Adventurous trait, felt extremely frustrated because her husband did not like to travel. He preferred to go fishing or just putter around in the garden, activities she found boring. I suggested she find a group of people or friends who would like to travel with her—people who shared her sense of adventure.

After her husband died, Meg, a High Adventurous woman in her seventies, sold their home and bought a boat and camper. She now travels the harbors and canals of England, and she stays at one place only until she feels ready to move on. She has no phone; her family waits for her to call them from time to time just to let them know where she currently is docked or parked.

Alan, an international marketing representative for a large company, told me he was just short of having traveled two million air miles. I asked him if he ever got fed up with all the travel required by his job. He said he would hate a desk job. "I'd be able to do it for a while," he explained, "but I would need the opportunity for change on a regular basis." Alan has extremely prominent cheekbones.

Individuals with this trait may confuse their adventurous spirit with the need to constantly be on the move and change residences. They are adaptable to change and enjoy their nomadic life.

The Adventurous trait can be seen in many of the Romany Gypsies, who adapted well to their lifestyle, as well as many other nomadic peoples including the Eskimo's. I spoke to an author who had written a book about the nomadic tribes of Iran, and without actually seeing them, I gave her what I thought would be a facial description of these people. She said the facial characteristics I offered described them exactly.

Adventurous

The Low Adventurous individual (no prominent cheekbones) may appear to be a "stick in the mud" to some people. These individuals are more content to stay at home. They do not feel the need to travel to distant places. They enjoy exploring areas close to home. To the High Adventurous person, this seems a dull life.

Famous Faces
Michelle Obama, Raquel Welch, James Coburn, Michael Fox

Relationships
High Adventurous people feel their less adventurous partner miss out on the excitement of life. They feel restricted if their partner does not have the same enthusiasm for travel. A Low Adventurous partner's life and interests can seem quite dull to a more adventurous individual.

If you are more adventurous, use your free time to travel or take up a hobby that gives you the variety you need. Keep in mind, though, that not everyone shares your enthusiasm for change. If this presents an issue in your relationship, discuss how you can arrange time together and still avoid the feeling of being tied to the home—especially if your partner is a "homebody."

Children
Children who have the Adventurous trait need constant change and excitement. If this need goes unsatisfied, they may get into mischief just for the thrill it provides, especially if they also have long ring fingers (High Risk Taking). Make sure their days include a variety of activities.

Sales

This trait has no applications in sales.

Careers

High Adventurous people enjoy the following jobs: flight attendant, travel agent, tour guide and international marketing or sales representative.

Chapter Eleven

The Ears

Music Appreciation

Rounded Outer Edge of Ear
Music appreciation

The Music Appreciation trait is determined by the roundness of the outer perimeter of the ear. The more rounded the ear, the greater a person's sensitivity to sound and rhythm. In fact, the structure of the ear simply provides a channel for intake of sound. The more rounded the outer edge of the ear, the greater its accuracy and reception of sound.

Sound has great power to evoke feelings and emotions. Some people find listening to music enjoyable, but they don't consider this activity a high priority. To others, music plays a huge part in their lives. For them, the sound of a bell, wind, or waves can be music to the ears. They hear music everywhere.

The High Music Appreciation trait provides a great asset to individuals who work as sound engineers or play or tune musical instruments. If they also have the Aesthetic Appreciation (straight eyebrows) trait, this heightens their sensual response to music. Individuals with this trait cluster are attuned to sound vibration and how music flows.

Andrew Lloyd Webber, a prolific composer who wrote and directed the musical *Cats*, provides a good example of the following cluster of traits: Aesthetic Appreciation (straight eyebrows), Music Appreciation (rounded out edge of ear), Design Appreciation (inverted V on eyebrow), and Dramatic Appreciation (flared eyebrows). Find a photo of him, and you'll see why he couldn't help but compose music.

The Aesthetic person (straight eyebrows) "feels" music rather than just hears it. Music becomes a part of his total sense of expression. Sometimes, the "ear for music," meaning the rounded outer edge of the ear, may not be present and still an individual becomes a professional or serious musician. Such people aim to create feeling with their music. When the inner helix or edge of the ear is also completely rounded, this indicates the individual has good pitch. If the ear is cupped out, this heightens their appreciation. They catch every sound. When the Aesthetic trait is combined with Critical Perception (outer corners of eyes lower than inner corners), these individuals make great music critics or sound mixers.

When the Music Appreciation trait is combined with fine hair (High Sensitive), you'll have a connoisseur of music. For these people, music is food for the soul. The fine-haired person enjoys softer music, while the coarse-haired (less sensitive) individual turns up the sound. This does not reflect musical preference, such as classic versus rock, just the volume of the music.

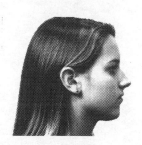

Music Appreciation

Rounded ears are noticeable in many professional soccer and tennis players. While I was at Heathrow airport, a team of young soccer players were waiting to board a plane. Without exception, they all had extremely rounded ears and short to medium legs (built to be on their feet). Having the Music Appreciation trait gives them an advantage in their sport, since a rhythm and smooth transitions exist in their movements, much like in music. Music Appreciation certainly also provides an asset for ice skating or dancing. People involved in these activities feel and express the music they hear better than those who do not have this trait. The next time you see someone running, check to see if the ears are rounded. Notice how smoothly they run.

A six-year-old girl who was sitting next to me suddenly got up and started to run. Watching her move was like looking at art in motion. She ran so smoothly; I noticed she definitely had the Musical Appreciation trait. Then a couple of boys who were at least two or three years older than her challenged her to a race. There was no competition. Much to their amazement, she just floated ahead of them. So if you have a child or teenager with this trait, encourage them to take up a sport or any activity that utilizes this innate ability, and don't limit their activities to those that are music-related.

I was sitting in a restaurant one day and happened to see a four-year-old boy having lunch with his father. I noticed he had the Music Appreciation trait, and after some thought, I decided to go up and speak to his father. As I approached him I said, "You have a musician in the family."

The man looked up at me in surprise and said, "Yes. My son is quite an accomplished trumpet player." I then explained what I do and said that his son inherited the trait from him. "Oh, yes," he said. "I am a drummer and play in a band." However, I had already noticed that the father also had the Music Appreciation trait.

My work is about making a difference in people's lives, hence my reason for sharing my observations with the father. I want to make sure parents are aware of their children's talents. Often, when I see children in other parts of the world where their talent is not encouraged, I think how much the child is missing, and in turn, how the countries are not utilizing and encouraging the talent in the next generation of their people.

Often, we see the Music Appreciation trait is handed down from parent to child. I was in an outdoor café located by a river and noticed a young girl with the Music Appreciation trait. I asked her parents if she was a musician. As it turned out, she played in a band at school. They asked me if I had heard their seventeen-month-old child play the mouth organ, I replied no; whereupon, they gave him the mouth organ, and he began to play a tune. It was quite amazing. The mother was a professional musician and played in an orchestra. Both she and her children had the C-shaped ears.

Jean, a student in my class in England, was traveling on a crowded, standing-room-only train to London. As she looked at the ears of the man standing next to her, she noticed he had the very trait we discussed in class the previous day: Music Appreciation. She plucked up courage and gave him a brief explanation of the class she was taking, and then she asked him if he played a musical instrument. He was somewhat amazed and said, "Yes, I did as a teenager."

Whereupon, she encouraged him to take it up again, and she suggested he would feel more balance in his life if he did so. Nothing more was said until they got off the train. The man turned around and commented, "I've been giving some thought about what you suggested. I've decided to take up playing my clarinet again. Thank you." Jean was thrilled. Just sharing her observation with the stranger inspired him to take up music again. It's about helping people reconnect with their talents and who they are by nature.

When the Music Appreciation trait is combined with Vocal Lines (two horizontal lines on the neck that run across the vocal chords), this enhances a singer's performance.

Famous Faces
Elton John, Andrea Bocelli, Sarah Brightman

Relationships
The Music Appreciation trait has no applications for relationships except if you enjoy music. Go to concerts you both enjoy. Sometimes people get so caught up in day-to-day life that they forget to take time out to go to musicals or concerts. It creates balance in one's life.

Children

Many autistic children and teenagers have the musical trait. They also have cupped-out ears (Acquisitive), so they hear sound more clearly. If you have a child that is autistic, explore various musical instruments with them. Find out which one interests them the most. Many young gifted children who are musically accomplished at an early age have this trait combination as well.

Sales

The Music Appreciation trait offers no application for sales. That said, if you notice your client has this trait, you might ask if they've been to any good concerts recently. Or if you know they enjoy music, you could have it playing in the background. This creates a personal touch. It's not all about business.

Careers

No careers relate directly to this trait other than the obvious ones, such as becoming a musician, a music instructor, or a sound engineer.

Pioneering Trend

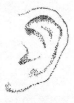

The Pioneer
Straight outer edge of ear

The straightness of the outside rim (helix) of the ear indicates the Pioneering Trend trait. Individuals with this trait do better working for themselves because working for other people curtails their independent spirit and makes them feel frustrated. Individuals who do not have this trait enjoy working for other people. Although you see them running successful businesses as well, they more easily adapt when working for others.

These are the Pioneers of new ideas, and they enjoy being on the leading edge of new technology. They like to explore new territory and start new projects. People who have this trait are visionaries with a burning desire to be the first to venture into new fields.

The greatest challenge for these individuals lies in staying focused and not getting too impatient when things don't happen quickly enough for them. They crave going beyond the horizon to find out what's next or new or different. They want "to tread where no one else has trodden before."

When this trait is combined with the ski jump nose (Ministrative), these individuals want to work for themselves. However, they must face the challenge of handling the financial side of the business. Once they master the business side or hire someone to do it for them, they can become successful.

A young Pioneering and Ministrative man who set up dance events struggled for a long time to make his business financially successful. He focused on creating a great space where people could dance and socialize without the usual bar scene. The concept worked, and the events became popular. However, the financial side posed a problem. He did not want to give up his dream, and the business was not generating the money needed to support his family.

The thought of working for someone else did not appeal to him, yet he had to decide whether to continue his events as a sideline or to simply acknowledge this as a passion, and do what it would take to make it financially successful. His Tenaciousness (protruding chin) helped him continue when others might well have given up. He made it into a business that eventually did support him and his family.

If an individual with the Pioneering Trend trait also has the trait cluster of Ministrative (ski jump nose), High Generosity (large lower lip) and Low Acquisitiveness (ears laid back against their head), they need to have a partner or hire someone to handle the financial side of the business.

Relationships

Running a business can prove time consuming. Be careful you don't neglect your partner or family over your business. If you choose a partner with a history of working for others, they may not understand your need to spend so much time on your business. A new business can take up a huge chunk of your time, especially if you are the only person running it. Get some help, so that you can spend some time with your family or your partner. Create balance in your life between work and play.

Children

If your children have this trait, you might want to keep a journal about the areas in which they show interest. This will help you see the thread that runs through their lives, which could provide an indicator of the direction they might want to pursue as a career.

Sales

The Pioneering Trend trait has no applications for sales.

Careers

The Pioneering Trend trait can be seen in all careers. Generally, individuals with the Pioneering Trend like to work for themselves, though. If they have the ski jump nose (Ministrative), they need to remember to charge the full price, or they may find it a struggle to make their business a financial success. Remember, just because you have a good product, it doesn't automatically make your venture financially successful.

Growing Trend

Personal Growth
Large earlobe

Individuals with large earlobes are naturally inclined to support others in their personal growth. This trait also indicates an interest in planting and maintaining living things.

Individuals with the trait combination of Construction (square forehead) and Growing Trend (large earlobes) like planting gardens, but they want someone else to maintain them. The same with indoor plants; they purchase them, but it takes a greater sustained effort for them to maintain and water the plants. In contrast, individuals with both an oval forehead (Conservation) and the Growing Trend trait cluster, love to plant gardens and enjoy maintaining them on a regular basis. Add a coarse hair (Low Sensitive) to this trait cluster, and you have individuals who love to be outdoors. For many people, gardening provides an escape from the daily stresses of life.

Earlobes increase in size as people get older. However, in most cases, the Growing Trend trait develops in the earlier years of a person's life.

Relationships
This trait does not present any relationship issues. If you or your partner have Growing Trend trait, you might enjoy gardening or volunteering for a cause.

Children
The Growing Trend trait does not create any issues with children. You might encourage them to plant some vegetables or have their own spot in the garden where they can grow plants.

Sales

This trait has no applications for sales.

Careers

People who have the Growing Trend trait make good forest rangers, geologists, biologists, archeologists, gardeners, psychologists, personal coaches, or environmental activists.

Idealistic

Opening of ear is lower
than the nostril

Low-set Ears
Head in the clouds, high standards

We can tell if someone is idealistic in nature by the placement of their ears. If the ears are low-set, meaning below the level of the nostrils, this facial feature indicates that an individual is more idealistic. When the ears are high-set, or higher than the level of the nostrils, this indicates that the person is more practical or more realistic. A special tool was designed in order to get an accurate reading for this trait. These tools are only available to people who complete the Advanced Face Pattern Recognition Course.

Idealism indicates the depth of feeling people hold about the ideals and standards they have chosen for themselves. It does not indicate the nature of their ideals or standards, but rather how dedicated they are to them. Idealistic people have high standards and can be very demanding. They become extremely disappointed when reality differs from what they think it should be.

Once Idealistic individuals completely set their focus on something, they tend to lose sight of what goes on around them. Combine this trait with Low Tolerance (close-set eyes), High Sensitive (fine hair), Builds confidence (narrow face), and Philosophical Tendencies (gaps between the fingers), this trait cluster identifies individuals who can totally get lost in their own dreams. They also may become so fanatical about their causes that things get out of hand. Examples of such extreme behavior have been seen in the Heaven's Gate cult, IRA, or Taliban, as well as in other deeply religious followers. Many of these individuals have these traits. These people get so caught up in the cause that they lose sight of what is real. I often suggest to some young ardent and Idealistic followers that they get out and travel. It helps them be more realistic if they can meet people in other parts of the world and learn about their lifestyles and perspectives on life.

Idealism can be directed toward hero worship, a ship to sail, a slum to clean, or an environmental cause. Individuals with this trait feel deeply hurt when one of their chosen "heroes" falls from the pedestal on which they placed them. Idealistic people do not like to "make do" or "compromise" where their principles, heroes, or standards are involved. They tend to become bitter when others fail them or if situations disappoint them by being less than perfect. Honest mistakes, errors, and imperfections constitute major catastrophes for which, in their eyes, no forgiveness exists.

Since Idealistic individuals dedicate themselves to high standards, they become tireless workers who give their all freely to the field or cause of their choice. In personal relationships, this trait can be very challenging; they often end up disappointed when their partner does not live up to their high expectations.

Idealistic

If you have the Idealistic trait, learn to accept others on their own terms, remembering that no one is perfect. Expect nothing more of others than that which they can give. Learn to acknowledge their achievements even though they may not come up to your high expectations. When you hear yourself saying, "If it can't be perfect, I want none of it," stop to think what you may be passing up.

Realistic (high-set ears) individuals are generally more practical and down to earth. They don't set their standards as high as Idealistic people. If you are more Realistic, you might want to set higher standards and not just make do or keep things status quo. Demand high standards from those working with you as well, and don't let others get away with less than the best.

Relationships

When Idealistic individuals enter into a relationship, they feel they have found the perfect mate with whom they will share the perfect life together. They put their partners and their relationships on pedestals, and they assume their significant other has the same high standards and expectations. Then they wonder why the relationships crash down around them, and they are left disappointed. Couples that include one Idealistic partner need to check in with each other to make sure they both have the same expectations.

Children

Idealistic children are dreamers; they sometimes live in a world of their own. They also want a perfect world and a perfect family. They often have a make-believe friend. If their parents get a divorce, this can devastate them.

Sales

Clients with this trait may be very demanding and will feel let down if the product or service does not come up to their expectations.

Careers

The Idealistic trait can be seen in ministers, psychologists, social workers, teachers, personal coaches, film directors, and writers, as well as in people working for a humanitarian or environmental cause.

Acquisitive

High Acquisitive
Ears cupped out

Low Acquisitive
Ears flat against the head

The High Acquisitive trait can be identified by the combination of protruding ears and oval forehead. Individuals with this combination of facial features collect everything—every nail, piece of paper, slice of wood, empty boxes, piece of string—you name it. They are loath to toss things out just in case it might be of use on another day. There comes a time when the piles get so high they almost take over the house.

Acquisitive

The High Acquisitive trait also indicates an individual's ability to hear sound well; the cupped-out ears make it possible for them to hear conversations three tables away. When people with such ears have their ears clipped back surgically, this takes away some of their natural ability to hear sound well. One woman said that her children thought her hearing was not as good after she had an operation to correct her protruding ears. Try cupping out your ears and listen to music or to someone talking, then press them back against your head, and notice the difference in your hearing. This will give you an idea of the difference between how a High Acquisitive and a Low Acquisitive person hears.

This trait also indicates the need to control, especially when combined with Low Tolerance (close-set eyes) and Conservation (oval forehead). Individuals with this trait cluster like to control people to the point where they actually stifle the other person's growth. One woman I met who had this trait cluster was so controlling that her daughter wanted nothing more to do with her. If these individuals feel unable to control you, in extreme cases, they may actually decide not have anything else to do with you. Now add tight skin, (the need to run things squeaky clean) to the trait cluster, and you have someone who may be an obsessive controller. Vladimir Putin has this trait cluster.

I met with a young teenager who was very controlling. I asked her how she would feel if someone were to control her. "I'd hate it," she said. My response was—now you know how it feels when you try to control others. However, High Acquisitive individuals with the above traits are also very good at controlling projects or programs. They are able to keep things together.

You often see this trait cluster in some of the top athletes. The tennis players Andy Roddick and Nikolay Davydenko have this trait.

Famous Faces
Vladimir Putin, Barack Obama—They will be good at controlling projects and programs also group discussion. Plus they both have tight skin over the frame of their face. This indicates they like to run a tight ship.

Relationships
When individuals have the Acquisitive trait, oval forehead (Conservation) and close-set eyes (Low Tolerance), they tend to be very possessive. They become very jealous if the other person in their life dares to pay too much attention to someone else. If their partners should get admiring glances or appear to be spending too much time with people of the opposite sex at a party, for instance, individuals with this trait combination perceive this as a threat to their relationship. Their philosophy is "My partner or my friend is mine and mine alone. He or she is not to be shared with anyone."

If you have the tendency to come across as controlling your partner, loosen up, or that other person in your life will feel stifled and may well leave you.

Children
No one should throw out another person's things before asking the owner's permission. This includes parents. Always ask your Acquisitive children first if they want to keep an item you want to throw away; don't just throw it out because you think it has no further use.

One father would go through his son's toys and discard what he thought was not needed. The child, who had protruding ears and the Acquisitive traits, was devastated, although he dared not tell his father. He would retreat into his own world, feeling hurt that something so special to him was thrown away.

Sales

If your client is very controlling, find ways for them to let go of the need to control every situation. Reassure them everything will be fine.

Careers

The Acquisitive trait along with Mechanical Appreciation (oval eyebrows) would be a good combination for careers in Project management, Event planning, Professional Organizers also interior designers. They would be good at controlling the projects.

Chapter Twelve

Lips

Concise/Verbose

Thin Upper Lip: Concise

Full Upper Lip: Verbose

The degree of how concise or verbose a person is can be determined by the fullness or thinness of the upper lip. The thinner the lip, the more concise their speech becomes; the fuller the upper-lip, this individual will be more verbose. The fullness of the lips is determined by comparing the size of the lips with the overall size of the face, not by comparing the size of their lips with that of other people's lips.

However, environmental situations affect the Concise/Verbose trait. If children have been constantly put down, or if they have been shown little affection, or lived in an abusive home, their lips become thin over time. I often see this trait in both men and women who have had a hard life or have been through a painful divorce that left them physically and emotionally drained. When the mouth is both thin and small in comparison with the whole design of the face, it may indicate extreme introversion or bottled-up feelings.

In California, they have a Three-Strikes Law, which dictates that a third felony conviction automatically sends a person to prison for life. This happened to a man whose third crime involved stealing a bicycle. When first interviewed by the television news program *60 Minutes*, his lips were full. A year later, he was interviewed again, and his lips had become so thin they had practically disappeared.

Concise

Individuals who have thin lips are more concise compared with those with fuller lips. At times, they may be perceived as terse and to the point. They dislike lengthy, drawn-out conversations; they turn such talk off in their head. During the 2000 United States Presidential Debates, Al Gore came across as wordy, whereas George Bush was more concise and to the point. The difference in these two men's facial features clearly shows Gore has the Verbose trait and Bush has the Concise trait. Concise people have the advantage of being able to give clear and easy-to-follow directions.

Concise people also often speak rapidly, and sometimes at length, particularly when they are nervous or are passionate about the topic about which they are talking. Many writers with this trait have shared that they have a hard time filling up the pages; they say what they have to say in just a few words.

If you are with a group of people and you notice one quiet person, ask that person open-ended questions to invite his or her opinion. Involve them in the discussion. Some Concise people are perceived as dull because they tend to be so quiet in social situations. They have lots to say, but they need encouragement to help them feel like speaking up. Once you accomplish this, they will talk at length about their latest project or the areas they feel passionate about, offering some new insight to the conversation.

If you have the Concise trait, try to embellish your conversation. Fill in your comments with more detail. If the person with whom you are meeting starts to talk at length, and you begin to feel frustrated, ask specific questions. Convey that you want to get directly to the point by saying, "Could you sum this up in just a few words?" Try to be patient with people who are more Verbose, and listen closely to the content of the conversation. You create a bond by acknowledging the other person's needs or issues.

If you have the Concise trait, be more open to expressing your feelings with people to whom you feel close to. They cannot second-guess how you feel toward them or what you are experiencing. This becomes especially important if you are also more Taciturn (teeth slant inward). You need to speak up.

A couple on the verge of divorce decided to have their personality profiles done. During the consultation, it was revealed that the husband, who had both a thinner upper (Concise) and lower lip (Low Automatic Giving), truly cared about his wife, but he had a hard time expressing his feelings to her. The last thing he wanted was a divorce. Since the husband had difficulty telling his wife how he felt even at that point, the consultant stood behind the husband and expressed for him how he truly felt about his wife. Afterward, she said, "I didn't know you cared, you never told me."

The couple's personology charts revealed many of the challenges they had been experiencing and demonstrated their personality differences. This gave them a tangible tool to work with and a way to appreciate each other's differences. It represented a turning point in their marriage. Today, they have a closer relationship and understanding of each other.

Nigel, a thin-upper-lipped British man, went to visit his young daughter. After arriving, a friend who had accompanied him asked, "Why don't you give her a hug, and show her that you care?" He responded, "I'm here, aren't I?" He thought his presence was a sufficient show of affection. It was difficult for him to express his feelings to his daughter.

I asked Nigel about his childhood. His told me he felt his parents never really wanted him. He did not recall his mother ever expressing her feelings verbally, and she seldom gave him a hug. His father was in the army, and he did not encourage expressing or discussing his personal feelings. In fact, you will notice many Englishmen have thin upper and lower lip. From birth, they are told to be tough, and they are not encouraged to express their feelings because it's not "proper."

I met a young man who was about seven years old, and his lips looked as if they had been sucked in. Previously, he had lived in some horrific foster homes. I gave him a brief reading, which he seemed to enjoy. Later, I was out sitting in the garden, and he came up to me and chatted away. My friend and his adopted mother observed the scene from inside the house and were amazed. They said he never spoke that much to anyone. Like many High Concise individuals, I think the fact that I talked to him about his good points made him feel safe to talk with me, and then he was able to communicate openly.

Famous Faces
Vladimir Putin, Russell Crowe, Mike Douglas

Relationships
If one of you has thin lips (Concise) and exposed eyelids (Bottom Line), try not to cut off your partner in mid-sentence; be patient and let them speak. If you also have the Introvert (teeth slant inward) trait, make sure you let your partner know what is going on inside yourself. He or she cannot guess what you are thinking or feeling. If your lips are fuller (Verbose) than your partner's lips, engage your partner in the conversation. Get them involved in the discussions.

If you go to an event, find someone who shares a common interest with your Concise partner; this makes their evening more enjoyable. Keep in mind that if they don't tell you they love you, don't take it personally. If you have the thin lips, be more open to sharing your thoughts and feelings with your partner.

Children
The Concise trait is not often seen in children. When children have this trait, it is an indicator that there is ongoing stress at home. When parents get divorced, this can have a huge impact on the children's lives. Also, if the children interpret their parents' behavior to mean they don't love them, they cope by keeping their feelings inside. In such cases, they pull their lips in, and they keep their feelings inside, thoughts, and

words to themselves. If this is the case with your children, encourage them in a gentle way to express themselves and to share their thoughts with you.

I received photos from Australia of a seventeen-year-old and an eleven-year-old whose parents were going through a divorce. The whites of their eyes were exposed under the irises, a facial feature that indicates long-term stress, and their lips were starting to form a thin wavy line. My heart went out to them.

Sales

If your customer has very thin lips, ask them open-ended questions, and remember to keep your conversation concise and to the point.

Careers

This trait is seen in people working in all careers

Verbose

If you ask Verbose people for directions, beware. They'll give you the complete tour between here and there. Ask them about their day, and they'll tell you every little detail. People with fuller lips have a natural ability to talk, and it takes little effort to start up and continue a conversation with them. Verbose individuals spontaneously add more interest to what they say. They will talk until the wee hours of the morning, especially if their companion also has full lips.

If you find yourself at the airport waiting for a delayed flight, look for someone with full lips; they will keep you thoroughly entertained. Time will fly by while you are talking with them.

I remember a recent flight I took to England. I tried mentally to put out the message that I wanted to sit next to a quieter person, hoping I'd create just that scenario. Well, the woman who sat down next to me had lips that couldn't have been bigger, and she hardly stopped talking during the entire flight. I gave her my book hoping that would keep her quiet, but that caused her to ask me many questions.

If you work with or meet a Verbose person, ask them questions that elicit a "yes" or "no" response. Or premise your questions by saying, "Could you briefly describe the situation?" You might try looking at your watch to indicate you only have so much time; otherwise, you might be spending hours with them.

On the positive side, the Verbose trait allows people to speak at length when required, for instance as a keynote speaker or a children's storyteller. They often have colorful and flowing speech that adds interest to their stories or speeches. They need to be aware of repetition, however, or listeners may become quickly bored.

Many people of African heritage tend to have fuller lips, and they are very expressive. However, some people within the culture have thinner lips as well, such as Reverend Jesse Jackson.

If you are more Verbose, be aware when you speak at length, or you may lose the attention of the person with whom you are talking to. Organize your thoughts before speaking. In a job interview, you could easily talk yourself into or out of a job. Give yourself some time to think things through. If you have this trait and find yourself being interviewed on radio or television, make sure you keep your responses brief and to the point. Airtime is expensive.

Be aware during long drawn-out conversations of whether or not the other person is still paying attention to you. Also, after such long conversations, the Concise individual may feel they have wasted precious time. This would also apply when you are talking to people who have the Low Analytical trait (exposed eyelid). They will be turned off by lengthy conversations. They dislike conversation for the sake of conversation itself. So those of you who love to talk, look for signals from other people, and keep it short and to the point when necessary.

Famous Faces: Full lips
Julia Roberts, Oprah Winfrey, Al Gore, James Coburn

Relationships
If your partner is more Verbose, try not to cut him or her off. Just be patient. Otherwise, your partner will think you're not interested in what he or she has to say. This could hurt your partner's feelings.

Children
Children with the Verbose trait can talk on and on. This can pose a problem in school as teachers may see them as talking too much and distracting others in class.

Sales
If you have the Verbose trait and you are meeting with a client who is more concise or wants the bottom line, keep your conversation brief and to the point. If you are a bottom-line person and your client is Verbose, be patient or say, "I only have so much time. Can we go over the most important things first?" If you don't, you will find your time is being wasted by long drawn-out conversations.

Careers
People in all careers have this trait.

Generous

Full Lower Lip
Very generous of their time and money

The fuller the lower lip in comparison with the size of the person's face, the more generous that person is by nature. Individuals with this trait give before being asked. They give more than required, including time, money, and possessions. They give without hesitation when they see others who have a greater need.

During the Christmas season, Ann, who had a full lower lip, was out on a present-buying spree in downtown San Francisco. As she left a store, she was approached by a homeless person who was begging for money. Her first response was not to give him anything, but she decided, "It's Christmas. I should give him some money. It might bring him a few moments of pleasure." Looking through her purse, she only found large bills. "Well, why not?" she thought.

The man was surprised at her generous donation, but gladly accepted it. A month later, she found herself in the same area and encountered the same homeless man. She hastily retreated into the store, not wanting to be approached by him again. However, the homeless man spoke to Ann's husband, who happened to be with her, and asked him to personally extend his gratitude to her. He said he had used the money she gave him to set up a street vending business.

An extremely Generous person buys a round of drinks for everyone when one has hardly enough money to pay for one's bare necessities. During the holiday season, he or she gives elaborate gifts to all his or her friends and family when he or she should be using the money to cover the bills. On the other hand, a person with the opposite of this trait is often seen as being very stingy. When a person has the following trait cluster: thin upper and lower lips, also convex nose, being very tight with money, and sees such giving as a complete waste of money.

One of my clients stated that she gives automatically in an almost obsessive manner to the point where she neglects her family. She donates so much time to other people's needs and causes that she has no time left for her family. She never saves because she sees no point. "Save the money for what?" she queries.

People with the Generous trait have a tendency to overextend themselves both in terms of their time and their money. They take on more than they can handle.

Also, Generous people may give automatically, but they often find it hard to receive gifts from others. For this reason, some people see them as ungracious recipients of gifts or simply not open to receiving.

If you are a Generous individual, learn when to say "no" before overextending yourself, and give only what you can reasonably afford in time, money, or possessions. Individuals who have the Generous trait with a combination of High Impulsiveness (protruding lips) and Low Acquisitiveness (ears flat against the head) as well, may give away everything they own.

If you have the Generous trait, allow others the pleasure of giving to you. Allow yourself to receive, and return the pleasure you felt from the act of receiving their gift; this returns the favor and gives them a gift as well. Express your appreciation. When you refuse gifts, or show lack of enthusiasm when being offered one, it can deeply hurt the giver's feelings. They may feel rejected. Imagine how you'd feel if someone rejected your generosity.

If you are less giving, learn to give to others without any strings attached. Give more of yourself in personal relationships and spend more time helping others who would benefit from your assistance. Express your feelings more often and on a deeper level. Surprise your significant other with a bouquet of flowers or a favorite bottle of wine. Open up and express your feelings to your children; tell them how much you care about them. Make sure you are available to them.

Famous Faces: Generous
Oprah Winfrey, Geri Halliwell, Jennifer Lopez

Relationships
If you are more generous by nature and have a hard time receiving gifts from your partner, remember to return the pleasure you experience to the person who is giving to you. Receive graciously, so they can enjoy giving to you.

Children
Children are naturally very giving, and they often share their toys with others. If they have the Acquisitive (cupped-out ears) trait though, they may not be as open to sharing. Encourage them to share. Ask them how it feels when their friends share toys with them. Help them to see situations from other people's point of view.

Sales

The Generous trait has no applications in sales. If your client offers you a gift in appreciation of you working with them, make sure you fully express your appreciation, and say that it has been a pleasure to work with them.

Careers

There are no specific careers for people who have this trait.

Taking Things Personally

Short space from the
top of the lip to the
base of the nose

Short Philtrum
Takes criticism very personally

To determine the tendency to take things personally, look at the length of the philtrum, the length between the nose and the lip. To evaluate this facial feature, the distance from the top of the lip to the base of the nose must be measured and compared with the length of the face. The shorter the philtrum, the more aware of their appearance a person becomes, and the stronger their desire to look good. This trait also indicates that these individuals take criticism extremely personally, thus its name—Taking Things Personally.

Individuals with this trait enjoy shopping for clothes and may have an extensive wardrobe. They have a natural ability to create attractive clothing combinations. This trait is often seen in designers, personal shoppers, and sales assistants in clothing or cosmetic departments.

Individuals with the Taking Things Personally trait may appear extremely vain and unable to go by a mirror without checking their appearance. They go to great pains to look good, appear successful, and only want to put their best foot forward. They fear criticism so much that they become fanatics about how they come across to others. Such was the case of a young man in a hotel lobby. He kept checking himself in the glass pictures and brushing his hands through his hair many times over—not that it changed his appearance. It just reassured him that his image was still intact since the last time he checked it a few minutes before. As you might have guessed, he had a short philtrum.

Individuals who have this trait are overly sensitive to criticism. Sharon believed criticism of her work meant she was a failure. When criticized, she felt completely destroyed, and she woke up in the night worrying about it. At such times, she would "go into an emotional hole" and feel "as small as a pea." As you may have guessed, in addition to the Taking Things Personally trait, she also had Low Tolerance (close-set eyes). Also Backward Balance (more head behind the ear compared to in front). With this trait cluster, she thought people must hate her when she missed a deadline. She took criticism to mean she was an absolute failure, and no one liked her. She took any slightly negative comment and over thought it to the point where it ended up taken completely out of context. After a while, she began to believe the criticisms. Her close-set eyes kept her focused until the problem became bigger than life—at least in her mind.

If you have this trait, try not to take things so personally. Clear up any miscommunications right away, and be ready to talk about what hurt your feelings. Be open to hearing and listening to the other person's response.

John who was very sensitive (fine hair) said he took criticism so personally that at times it paralyzed him. He received the most criticism about his writing, which created a block for him when he was a young child. During the times when his parents argued with each other, he escaped to his room and wrote stories. Both his parents and teachers heavily criticized his writing. They told him he was wasting his time. However, he never gave up his dream. After some years, he became a successful writer. If you know of a child or adult who has an interest in writing, support them with your encouragement. Who knows, they could become a successful writer or journalist.

Geoffrey Thompson, author of **The Great Escape**, had always wanted to become a writer. As a child, he was never given the support or encouragement to follow his dream. All he could hear was the criticism. Thus, it wasn't until later in his adult life that he made his dream a reality. He is now the author of many books, and he has directed a number of films.

Famous Faces
Steven Spielberg, Tom Cruise, Halle Berry, Nancy Pelosi

Relationships
If your partner has the Taking Things Personally trait, he or she could take a harmless comment or remarks made by you and feel extremely hurt. Make sure you clear up differences right away.

Children
Children with the Taking Things Personally trait may take negative remarks very personally. If they also have close-set eyes (Low Tolerance), they may focus on what was said for hours or days. Try to find out what was said or what happened; they may have gotten the comment out of context.

Sales

This trait has no specific applications in sales.

Careers

You will see this trait in every career.

Dry Sense of Humor

Long space from
the top of lip to
base of nose

Long Philtrum
Dry sense of humor

A long space from the top of the lip to the base of the nose, or a long philtrum, indicates a person with the Dry Sense of Humor trait. In stark contrast to the Takes Things Personally trait, an individual with the Dry Sense of Humor trait takes criticism with a grain of salt. In fact, criticism tends to run off them just like water off a duck's back. They appear impervious to how other people feel about them.

As noted in the name of this trait, these people have an extremely dry sense of humor; not everyone gets their jokes. At times, they unintentionally come across as sarcastic. Dry humor may be amusing to some people, but it can have devastating effects on others, especially when the remarks are cutting or sarcastic. This trait can present a challenge, and when out of control, it can shatter relationships.

A man went to visit his parents, whom he hadn't seen for some time. One of his parents immediately said something sarcastic about his appearance. Throughout his stay, the parents repeatedly directed cutting remarks toward him, until he just wanted to leave. If you have the Dry Sense of Humor trait, be aware of the effect your sarcasm has on other people, particularly those with fine hair (Sensitive) and a short philtrum (Takes Things Personally).

Such was the case with a member of my family who has this trait. I greeted him with a big hug. His arms remained down by his side. I said to him, "Come on . . . you can give me a hug." He sarcastically responded with a smirk on his face, "Oh, I'd never be able to get my arms around you."

In the kindest tone I could muster, I said, "I am sure you did not intend to be offensive. However, some people could really feel hurt by that remark. You need to be more sensitive to other people's feelings."

Later that week, he actually did compliment me. To me, this demonstrated his regret about the remark, and he was more aware of how his comments may be effecting others.

If a person with the Dry Sense of Humor trait hurts your feelings, clear up the situation right away in a manner that brings positive results; try not to end up in a shouting match or an argument that leaves lingering resentment. These people do not hear themselves being sarcastic. In general, they do not intend to hurt anyone.

Also, people who have the dry humor trait often come across as being very sarcastic toward their families. One husband said he often ended up the target of his wife's sarcasm. To her, the use of sarcasm did not represent a big deal. She felt her husband overreacted to her comments. She had coarse hair (Less Sensitive) and a Dry Sense of Humor (long philtrum), so sarcastic remarks did not affect her quite as quickly. Her husband tried to explain how her remarks embarrassed him in front of people. She responded, "They didn't embarrass me." This was one of the traits that many of the most successful women in England had in common. They are able to handle the flack that comes their way. They don't let sarcastic or critical remarks get to them. As the saying goes "thick skin" which in their case really helped them brush off negative comments or remarks.

A seventy-five-year-old man sent me his photo, and the first thing I noticed was his Critical Eye (outer corner lower than inner corner) and Dry Sense of Humor. Two months after I completed his personology assessment and CD, he wrote to me. Apparently, prior to his chart arriving, he had a huge fall out with his fifty-year-old daughter and had severed the relationship. Then he listened to the CD with a detailed description of his assessment. He heard himself clearly for the first time. He called his daughter and apologized, and now they have a great relationship. He had no idea how he was coming across to other people. Those who have the Dry Sense of Humor trait do not hear the sarcasm in their voice; it's something that has always been there. Many of them grew up in a sarcastic family, so hearing this type of language and tone of voice seems natural to them.

People who have the Dry Sense of Humor trait are more concerned with getting the job done, rather than how they look while doing so. When they dress in the morning, they would much rather put on comfortable clothes than get all dressed up. Additionally, they are less interested in current clothing trends. For these reasons, they are the personal shoppers' dream clients because so much improvement can be achieved with their wardrobes. These individuals get so wrapped up in what they're doing that how they look becomes the last thing on their mind.

If you have the Dry Sense of Humor trait, you might want to hire a personal shopper when you buy clothes; this will save you time and money in the long run. In addition, hiring someone to help you choose your clothes makes the shopping experience an enjoyable one rather than one of necessity. This more casual approach to shopping is modified when the skin seems to be very tight on the frame of the face (like things to be neat and tidy). These people enjoy dressing well but not to the point of being vain.

Famous Faces
Ozzy and Sharon Osbourne, George Bush, Andy Rooney, Mick Jagger

Relationships
If you have the Dry Humor trait and the Critical (outer corner of eye lower than inner corner) trait, be careful you don't come across as being too sarcastic toward your partner or children. The constant sarcastic remarks can be devastating.

Children
Your children may have inherited this trait too. If so, talk to them about how their sarcastic remarks could hurt other people, especially their friends or fellow students at school.

Sales
If you have the Dry Sense of Humor trait, keep it out of the sales process. If you see this trait in your client, don't take their sarcasm personally.

Careers
This trait can be seen in people working in all careers. If you have the Dry Sense of Humor trait, however, be careful about making sarcastic remarks to your coworkers. This could end up causing hard feelings. And be sure not to speak sarcastically to your boss.

Impulsiveness

Protruding Lips
Says and acts without thought

A person's tendency toward Impulsiveness can be observed from the side profile, and it is indicated by how much the lips protrude past the ridge of the nose near the center of the eyebrows. To determine this facial feature, first make sure the head is level. Then take a pencil, and line it up with the ridge of the nose. When looking at the profile of the face, notice if the lips project forward in front of the pencil or recede behind it. If the lips protrude, this indicates an impulsive nature. High impulsive individuals will say and do things in the moment they may regret later. They act without thinking, which often gets them into trouble.

Those with High Impulsiveness tend to interrupt conversations and may bring up something from out of the blue. They often speak without thinking about the impact their words have on others. These people are also impulsive spenders, especially if accompanied by a ski jump nose (Ministrative).

The Low Impulsive people tend to be more calculated in thought and action. They act deliberately, and they are not prone to quick or impetuous decisions. People with Low Impulsiveness and Sequential Thinking (vertical forehead) take time to consider major buying decisions. Do not try to rush these people into making a purchase; give them time to think through their decision.

If you have the High Impulsiveness trait, look before you leap, or you may regret your decisions. Learn not to interrupt conversations. Pay attention to what is being said by others, and allow other people to complete their comments or responses during conversations. Count to ten before you say anything, and leave more of your thoughts unspoken.

If you have the Low Impulsive trait, do something spontaneous for once, and see how it feels.

Famous Faces: High Impulsive
Raquel Welch, Bill Gates, Halle Berry

Relationships
If you have the High Impulsive trait, before committing yourself to a long-term relationship, look at all the pros and cons first, and then make a decision. Otherwise, your impulsive nature may get you into situations that you might regret later.

Children
Impulsive children are extremely spontaneous, and they may get involved in situations before really thinking them through. You might remind them to think first and act afterward.

Sales
If your client has the High Impulsive trait, he or she could be an impulse buyer and have a change of mind later. Make sure the client is committed to his or her decision to buy. This will avoid wasting time on returned products.

Careers
People with the High Impulsiveness trait enjoy and are good at jobs as paramedics, fire fighters, public speakers, radio and TV broadcasters, auctioneers, interpreters, and salespeople.

Optimism/Pessimism

Optimistic
Upturned mouth

Pessimistic
Down-turned mouth

You can recognize the Pessimism trait by the downward turn of the outer corners of the mouth. Another environmental trait, it develops over time by the muscles constantly being pulled down at the corners of the mouth. This facial feature usually reflects the inner negative chatter that goes on in the pessimist's head. This trait is mostly seen in adults whose life circumstances have taken a toll on their faces; thus, it is most noticeable in older people.

I once met a business owner whose mouth was turned down at only one corner. When her business was going well, she was afraid she would not be able to fill her orders. When no orders were coming in, she thought the business was going to fail. Her business was, in fact, quite successful. No matter how much the sun was shining on her that day, she always saw a storm ready to come in. That attitude kept the corners of her mouth pointing in two directions.

Pessimists look at the dark side of life, and they are hard to please. Their thoughts immediately go to what is not working, or they look at the worst-case scenario. With some coaching, they can change.

If you have the Pessimistic trait, ask yourself what it would feel like to spend time with constantly negative people. How would you feel? Would you want to seek out their company? What would you advise them? Then consider what steps you can take now to look at the more positive side of life. When you find yourself going into negative self-talk, close your eyes, and simply empty out your thoughts. Or for example, if you find yourself driving your car and negative thoughts are pouring into your head, simply decide not to flow where they are going. Once you practice ways to let negativity go, you will be able to do it instantly.

That said, you must do more than simply "let go" of negative thoughts; the mind abhors a vacuum. You must learn to replace the empty space with positive thoughts, or the mind simply reverts to negativity again. This can be exaggerated if you also have the Critical (outer corner of eye lower than inner corner) trait. Constant criticism often pulls down the outer corners of the mouth.

Individuals with both the Pessimism and High Critical traits can be hard on themselves, so much that after a while, they wear themselves down and others with them. If this trait is combined with Backward Balance (more head in back of ears), people with these traits tend to bring up the negative things that happened in the past over and over again. This further contributes to their pessimism, reinforcing an already tainted attitude that believes, "This is the way it has always been and always will be." I have noticed that the Pessimistic trait, is often observed in people who have the Critical Trait (outer corner of eye lower than inner corner). Nothing is ever good enough, the down turned mouth reflects this inner chatter.

Relationships
If one of the partners in a relationship has the High Pessimism trait, and is therefore, constantly pessimistic and critical, it will wear their partner down. If you have this tendency, think about how it would feel if your partner constantly put you down or put a damper on your ideas. We all have choice, and in relationships or with family, we need to show understanding and support of each other; otherwise, the relationship falls apart.

Children
We do not see the Pessimistic trait in children; they usually are fairly positive by nature.

Sales
If your client has the Pessimistic trait, place an emphasis on what works and how the product or service you are selling will help them. They will need to be convinced.

Career
This trait can be seen in all careers. If you have the Pessimistic trait, try to look on the positive side of life. Focus on what works, rather than on what doesn't, or you will bring down the enthusiasm of others around you.

Chapter Thirteen

The Hair

Coarse Hair

Less sensitive

Fine Hair

Extremely sensitive

Do you have fine, medium, or coarse hair? Just like your facial features, your hair suggests an aspect of your personality.

The texture of the hair determines individuals' sensitivity to sound, touch, taste, and feelings. A micrometer, which measures the thickness of a single strand of hair near the ear, is used to determine this trait. The thickness also can be estimated by feeling the hair, but this method is less accurate. The finer the hair, the greater a person's sensitivity; the coarser the hair, the longer it takes for situations to get under that person's skin.

Fine Hair

Many people assume that people with African or Asian heritage have coarse hair. However, their hair has a wide range of textures, just like other ethnic groups.

Individuals with fine hair are extremely sensitive. Their feelings are easily hurt, and they are sensitive to loud noises or anything rough and coarse.

I have baby-fine hair, which means I have the Sensitive trait. How do I handle sensitivity? When I find myself in a situation where I feel hurt or I see myself as over reacting, I remind myself not to be so sensitive. I try to just let go of whatever is bothering me and not to overreact even if I feel hurt.

If people who have the Sensitive trait also have close-set eyes (Low Tolerance), they can wallow in their hurt feelings for days, thinking only about what someone said or did to them. To others, these Sensitive souls seem to overreact. One very sensitive client told me that if her parents simply looked at her when she did something wrong, she would shrivel up inside. Loud music, noisy machinery, the grating of a knife across a plate, or someone talking loudly really bothers Sensitive people. If the noise continues, they become quickly irritated.

On the phone, fine-haired people's voices sound soft, particularly if they also have a narrow face (Builds Confidence). When giving a talk or making an announcement, they need to remember to project their voice, so they are heard.

Chris, a woman with fine-hair, felt passionate about her work as a speaker, but she wondered why her message was not getting across. As I coached her, I was able to point out she had a soft voice, and she didn't express her emotions in her face. I suggested she speak up and use more expression in her voice and in her face when she made a presentation. Plus she needed to wear stronger colors to support her verbal and visual message. Despite her Sensitive trait, her message now gets across more powerfully, and her passion is clearly communicated when she speaks.

Fine Hair

All through Ruth's life, she had been accused of being overly sensitive and was told by both her British mother, and later in life, her husband to "Toughen up... It's not proper to show your feelings." I noticed her fine hair. When I explained the High Sensitive trait to her, Ruth felt she was understood for the first time. Over the years, she had withdrawn, and she felt the only way to cope was to keep her feelings inside. This could be seen by her thin lips (Concise), which indicated she had held back her anger and frustration for years. With some coaching, she was able to manage her tendency to be overly sensitive and emotionally repressed. All she needed was the validation that someone understood her natural responses.

Fine-haired individuals enjoy quality, whether that comes in the form of fine pieces of furniture or delicate china. They appreciate elegant dining and as well as traveling in comfort. If you take them camping, make sure you make it a comfortable experience; otherwise, stay in a local bed and breakfast or hotel instead.

Famous Faces
J. K. Rowling, Katie Couric, Kiefer Sutherland, John Grisham

Relationships
Many couples who are on the opposite poles of the Sensitivity trait have told me that the differences in their personal sensitivities posed challenges in their relationship. The person with fine hair sees the coarse-haired partner (Less sensitive) as uncaring and insensitive to his or her feelings or emotions. On the other hand, the coarse-haired individual sees the partner as being overly sensitive and too needy. The coarse-haired

partner's attitude toward his or her fine-haired partner seems to indicate that the other should "toughen up" and "not be such a wimp."

Children
Children who have fine hair will be very sensitive to criticism they receive from fellow students or family members. Parents need to be there to help them get through those moments.

Sales
If you are in a noisy place, suggest going somewhere quieter. Otherwise, your fine-haired client will find it difficult to stay focused on the discussion.

Careers
There are no specific careers for people who have the High Sensitive trait, although this trait is often seen in chefs, wine connoisseur, or in people choosing any career that benefits from their more sensitive qualities.

Coarse Hair

People with coarser hair may come across as being less sensitive. It takes a lot more for situations to get under their skin. They have feelings, but they do not come to the surface quite as quickly compared with people with finer hair. It takes a lot more stimulus to elicit a response from these folks. In general, coarse-haired individuals also are less sensitive to pain. They find Sensitive people very annoying.

Most politicians have coarser hair and have the Low Sensitive trait. This gives them an added "coat of armor" against the inevitable criticism they receive. Bill Clinton, Gordon Brown, Colin Powell, and Pakistani President Pervez Musharraf all have coarse hair. Many corporate CEOs and professional athletes have this trait too. They are constantly coming under criticism, and they often need to deal with extreme crises. While a fine-haired individual could handle these situations and pressures, it would eventually wear them down. Coarse-haired individuals weather the stress better and for longer periods of time.

Coarse Hair

Coarse-haired people tend to be aggressive in sales. During a networking event, a woman with coarse hair volunteered her assistance in selling products at my booth. She became quite excited with the results she generated. She kept punching my arm saying in a loud voice, "See, how good I am." By the end of the afternoon, my arm was sore. I was embarrassed by her brashness and aggressive selling style.

Individuals with coarse hair enjoy things on a larger scale, whether it is loud music, boisterous laughter, strong sensations, or relationships with lots of intensity. They love the outdoors, camping, and the extreme elements of the sun, wind, rain, and snow. If they also have olive green eyes, this adds to their enjoyment of outdoor activities. They love the ruggedness of the outdoors. A client with this Low Sensitive trait told me that when work became too stressful, she found camping helped her forget all her troubles. She was able to get a better night's sleep in the outdoors than at home. If you have this trait, consider joining a hiking group that shares your passion for the outdoors.

People whose hair contains a wide range of textures find themselves switching from one end of the sensitivity spectrum to the other. One moment they thoroughly enjoy loud music, and suddenly, they find the noise level unbearable. One such woman I met loved both extremes, but it's only when she was able to handle them. Sometimes, she found herself walking out of rock concerts because the music was too loud; the previous weekend, the sound level didn't bother her. This really confused her boyfriend, who, of course, looked forward to attending the events. Her unpredictable mood changes became a sore point in their relationship.

Famous Faces: Coarse Hair
Tony Blair, Prince Harry

Relationships
In relationships, it is ideal for both people to have similar hair texture. If the partners have wide differences, this opens the way for many more misunderstandings and hurt feelings. Should one person have coarse hair (Low Sensitive) and the other fine (High Sensitive), the finer-haired person may perceive the other as being rough and loud. In turn, the coarser-haired individual could find his or her partner overly sensitive and complaining. Even though couples have these differences, it doesn't mean the relationship won't work. They just need to be more aware of each other's needs and preferences.

Children
Fine-haired children get their feelings hurt quickly. Knowing this about your children helps you understand them better. For example, a young girl with fine hair ran off to her room whenever her feelings were hurt. Her mother always wondered why her daughter suddenly disappeared, unaware that she was upset. This was the child's way of coping with her emotions.

If your children have coarse hair, teach them to be more understanding toward more sensitive children. Teach them to modulate their voices and not to be so rowdy around others with finer hair.

When parent and child have significant differences in this trait, the coarse-haired parent needs to be aware of the effect he or she has on the fine-haired child. For example, a coarse-haired father may see his fine-haired son as behaving like a wimp. He'll want the son to "toughen up" and "act like a man." He needs to avoid negative comments that can harm the child. One High Sensitive little girl retreated into her shell because her stepfather acted aggressively toward her. He was unaware of his effect on her. Once he became aware of his stepdaughter's nature, he took a softer approach.

It is particularly important to become aware of these differences if the parent is a stepfather or stepmother or if the child is adopted or if you are a foster parent.

Sales

If you work in real estate sales and your client has fine hair, show them homes in quieter neighborhoods. Houses on cul-de-sacs are ideal for them. To determine if your client has fine hair, notice how the fine hair tends to lay close to the head, rather than having a more springy texture, which would indicate coarse hair.

Careers

People with fine hair do well in careers such as wine tasting, gourmet cooking, homeopathy, or any career where sensitivity to taste or smell is beneficial.

CHAPTER FOURTEEN

THE HANDS

Risk Taking

High Risk Taker
Ring finger longer
than index finger

Calculated Risk Taker
Ring finger shorter
than index finger

Although hands do not make up part of the face, when doing a personology profile on a person, it's helpful also to look at certain aspects of a person's hands. They offer an amazing amount of information about a person's personality as well.

Upon arriving at the Seattle airport, I went in search of a taxicab. I had hardly stepped out of the airport when a cab came zooming up to me. *That was quick*, I thought. I got into the cab, and off we went at high speed. I took one look at the driver's hands as he clutched the steering wheel; I tightened the seat belt and grabbed something to hold on to. From his hands alone, I knew we were about to break all speed records. My driver also appeared to be sleepy, although that did not seem to slow him down. This added to my anxiety. I felt a great sense of relief as I stepped out of the cab to the safety of the hotel driveway. I left him with the parting words, "Slow down."

Risk Taking

The Risk-Taking trait is determined by the length of the ring finger compared with the length of the index finger. This feature is best viewed with the palms of the hands facing toward you. If you are looking at your own hands, stand in front of a mirror and hold them up with the palms toward the mirror. The fingers need to be touching each other and the knuckles straight.

If the ring finger is longer than the index finger, this indicates a person who enjoys taking risks. Risk gives these individuals a natural high, a rush of adrenaline. If a difference exists between the finger measurements of the two hands, this indicates that, at times, the person has a more cautious side to their nature and, at other times, they enjoy taking risks.

If both ring fingers are shorter than the index fingers, this indicates a person who is naturally more cautious, and he or she prefers to take calculated risks. Such people look at all the odds before taking chances.

Risk taking could be anything from adrenaline-releasing physical activities, like skydiving, to more intellectual and passive ventures, such as speculating on the stock market or gambling. Sometimes, they are willing to risk everything without considering the consequences. Such was the case of one couple, where the husband was an impulsive gambler and lost everything they owned, including the house. The marriage suffered the consequences of his High Risk-Taking trait and a divorce followed.

On my way to the airport, I asked my taxi driver why he enjoyed living in Las Vegas. He said he loved gambling. I asked him to hold up his hands—one at a time, so at least one hand remained on the wheel. Sure enough, his ring fingers could not have been any longer. Gambling gave him the "buzz" in his life; it made living seem more worthwhile. To the conservative person, it would seem ridiculous to put one's finances and security at risk. To this taxi driver, taking such risks simply represented part of his nature. However, he did have the power of choice.

When Risk Taking is combined with a sloped-back forehead (Objective Thinking), individuals with this combination love driving fast cars. One client I met said his dream was to own a hot rod. When Mark was sixteen, he loved racing cars around the fields, and he later won many car racing competitions. After a serious accident, he was laid up for months. Once he had recuperated, he immediately began racing again. Racing cars constituted an exhilarating experience, requiring a lot of focus. It gave him a "rush of adrenaline" unlike anything else. So like any addiction, he had to keep seeking out that high—especially when his job didn't provide any real stimulation.

Mark also loved trading on the commodity market. He stated, "When the time's right, you just do it." In one year alone, he bought twenty-two flats in London, betting on the market going up. He invested a ton of money in real estate. The thrill of risking everything drove him; without that thrill, he felt life would be extremely dull. He did not look at his ventures as real risks because he felt he had the ability to manage them. Individuals with the High Risk-Taking trait enjoy living on the edge of life.

One man I interviewed who had the High Risk-Taking trait said he had an addiction to spending. However, once he made the purchase whether it was expensive clothes, a car or whatever took his fancy, grief sets in because the excitement of spending disappeared. He got a buzz from making risky purchases, but the feeling only lasted for a short time and then left him empty. This man worked as a professional football player. He enjoyed taking physical risks as well; for him, the game represented opportunities to take chances. Additionally, he risked on a personal level by flirting excessively; he perceived this behavior as a game too. He had little fear of anything.

Ann, another person with the Risk-Taking trait, loved to invest her money in high-risk investments. She took the attitude "No skin off my back. Just go for it." Her husband was a great risk taker, enjoyed taking financial risks. This presented a challenge to their financial planner. For them, money had no value other than for making large purchases.

Ann told me about a time when she and her husband went white water rafting. She fell out, and she was caught under the raft by her life vest. Her husband, who could not swim, also fell out of the raft. Even that didn't dampen their enthusiasm. They went right back the next day and continued the rafting trip. Another time, she and her husband went hiking in the mountains. As they were coming back down from their trip, she saw fresh mountain lion prints along with their own. Rather than feeling scared, the experience thrilled Ann.

Risk Taking for Eva, whose ring finger was longer than her index finger, and who loved bungee jumping, gave her a total feeling of complete surrender. When she bungee jumped off a bridge, she described the experience as "awesome." Once the element of fear had passed, however, she tried in every way to get a new experience, a new high. She did not know whether she would live through her next "adventure," but she thought, "Why not try anyway? Just let go." She found Risk Taking exhilarating; it tapped into her aliveness. She loved to coach others to take risks too.

Many firemen I have talked to say the risk involved in their job gives them a rush. They like this aspect of their job.

If you have the Risk-Taking trait, consider how the risk you plan could affect other people's lives. Participate in a sport or other activities that satisfies your need to take chances. Do not expect people with the Low Risk-Taking trait to eagerly embrace your passion for risk.

If you enjoy gambling, make sure you keep within your budget, particularly if you have family responsibilities. Many relationships have been affected by out-of-control gambling. Ask yourself, "Is it worth the gamble to lose what I have?"

Famous Faces
Many of the people who engage in sports or any other high-risk activities will have the Risk-Taking trait. This would also apply to politicians and top business executives.

Relationships

If your partner is more cautious by nature, explain to him or her what the risk entails. Go over in detail what to expect; this may help your partner relax and be more willing to take the risk with you. If you are the risk taker, be careful when making any kind of investment. Get a second opinion.

Children

In the town where I live, there are several steps that connect one street to another. One day, as I was walking down the steps, some boys between the ages of eight and twelve rushed down on their skate boards. The youngest one crashed at the bottom. Seeing that he wasn't hurt, I said to him, "Let me look at your hands." "No," he said. I asked him again, and again he refused. His friends then said, "Show the lady your hands." Sure enough, he had the Risk-Taking trait. I then looked at all the other boys' hands, and I was able to point out that they all were risk takers.

Then to my amusement, they saw a man walking up the steps toward them, and they ran up to him and said, "Excuse me, sir. Can we see your hands?" After examining his upturned hands, they all agreed, "You're not a risk taker." In response the man said, "You got that right." I am sure they spent the rest of their morning checking out all the hands in town!

If your children have the Risk-Taking trait and enjoy Risk-Taking activities, make sure they have the training needed prior to their participation. At least, you will feel more relaxed about what they are doing. Plus the chances of them becoming injured will, hopefully, be reduced.

It is important to recognize the Risk-Taking trait in teenagers, or they may direct this need in a negative direction, such as toward buying and selling drugs, racing cars, or shoplifting. Channel their energies into sports or other activities that offer them an element of risk.

The reward for those with the Risk-Taking trait comes in the form of the exhilarating experience itself. Low Risk-Taking parents, who have a more cautious nature, may find this hard to understand. When they recognize and support their children's needs, however, it will help them guide their children through the more challenging years.

Sales

If your client tends to be a big risk taker, you'll find them easier to work with when a project requires a large investment. They won't be as hesitant. Someone who doesn't have the High Risk-Taking trait will be more cautious about investing in a new product or service.

Careers
No specific careers exist for people who have the Risk-Taking trait. However, people who have this trait might find it an asset in jobs where large investments are made.

Low Risk Takers

When the ring finger is the same length or shorter than the index finger, these individuals take more calculated risks. They take a conservative approach. People with the Low Risk-Taking trait first consider all aspects of a situation before taking a chance. A risk for these people could consist of changing jobs, living in a new city, making investments, or participating in a new activity. The activities they perceive as risky may appear dull to those who are risk takers. The calculated risk takers do not enjoy activities that take them out of their own comfort zone. They like to check all the odds first before taking risks.

If you have a more cautious nature, and you are contemplating doing something in which some element of risk exists, familiarize yourself with what it entails. This will help you approach the situation with more confidence. Don't dampen the enthusiasm of people who seek the unknown with your cautiousness.

Relationships

If you are the Low Risk-Taking partner in the relationship, be more willing to take risks with your partner, especially the ones that feel a bit more comfortable for you. Don't put a damper on your partner's need to take physical risks. If your partner insists on a financially risk, encourage him or her to get a second opinion.

Children

If your children are hesitant about taking even the smallest risk, go through the process with them in little steps. This will help to take the fear out of taking risks.

Sales

Customers with the Low Risk Taking trait will appear more cautious. Just take them through the steps and reassure them their investment is well protected—assuming, of course, that it is.

Careers

This trait does not relate to any careers although you may find a number of successful business owners may well have the Risk Taking trait. At times they may risk all.

Hand Dexterity

High Hand Dexterity
Three middle fingers
similar in length

Low Hand Dexterity
Three middle fingers
different in length

Dexterity is determined by the three middle fingers. With your palms facing you and the fingers together, take a look at your three middle fingers. If they are similar in length, this indicates High Hand Dexterity. To accurately determine this trait, a specially designed tool was made for measuring Hand Dexterity.

People with this trait have an innate skill to grasp and manipulate objects effectively. If the ends of the fingers also are square, this adds to their skill. Such people are natural handymen. We see this trait in car mechanics, carpenters, sculptors, massage therapists, dentists, and artists. We also see it in musicians if they have the Music Appreciation (a rounded outer edge of ear). If you are not a natural handyman and, instead, have the Low Hand Dexterity trait, hire someone else who loves to do that work.

The innate ability to work with one's hands is heightened if a person also has fine hair (Sensitive), Music Appreciation (a rounded outer edge of ear), and Aesthetic Appreciation (straight eyebrows). These people find the hands-on experience meditative.

I asked a dentist who had these traits why he chose dentistry as a career. He answered, "I enjoyed working with my hands, and this was a profession where I could generate a reasonable income doing just that."

If your children have High Hand Dexterity, buy them toys that require they use their hands, to build on their natural skills. Support and acknowledge them when they achieve results when using their hands, even though those results may not come up to your expectations. If Johnny has an innate ability to do well in arts and crafts and Sean finds it's a struggle to do half as well, encourage Sean, who likely has the Low Hand Dexterity trait, into another activity where he can excel. Be sure to point out the merit of each child's ability to both children.

Relationships

This trait does not present an issue within relationships.

Children

If your children have High Hand Dexterity, sign them up for arts and crafts classes. If they also have the Music Appreciation (a rounded outer edge of ear) trait, they might enjoy playing the piano or guitar. Let them decide which instrument they would like to play. Rent the instrument before buying it; this could save you some money, since their desire to play might just be a passing interest.

Sales

This trait offers no application in sales

Careers

People with the High Hand Dexterity trait should explore careers as massage therapists, chiropractors, physical therapists, dentists, hair stylists, carpenters, construction workers, auto mechanics, and musicians. They also will enjoy the following hobbies, which can just as easily also be applied to different types of careers: woodworking, sewing, stenciling, quilting, pottery, sculpting, jewelry-making, painting, or mosaics.

Intense Feelings and Emotions

Explosive Emotions and Anger
Thumb comes up to first joint on finger

When the thumb reaches the first knuckle of the index finger, this may indicate explosive feelings and emotions. To observe this feature, the fingers must be straight and touching each other. The thumb should be resting against the index finger. Make sure the knuckles are straight; just glancing at someone's hands when they are slightly bent may give the wrong appearance.

Individuals with this trait experience anger or other emotions that come quickly to the surface, exploding in the moment and taking people by surprise. Yet the emotions go as quickly as they come. As people mature, they often learn to hold back their anger; they realize it can get them into trouble. Yet individuals with this trait may strike out at whatever infuriates or threatens them. Often, the target of this anger lies within the family. However, as with all traits, they do have conscious choice about how to handle their reactions.

The Intense Feelings and Emotions trait has a lot to do with having control. So if the situation gets out of hand, and people are not doing what they were told to do or agreed to do, people who have this trait quickly find their emotions come rushing to the surface.

Sally, a person with the Intense Feelings and Emotions trait, had prepared a stew for the evening meal, which had been simmering on the stove for a long time. Her well-intended mother-in-law thought the stew was done and turned off the heat beneath it. This caused Sally to feel extreme anger. She perceived the action of her mother-in-law as one of interference. In a rage, she took the stew off the stove, and she poured it out on the garden. This provides a good example of how this trait manifests when a person cannot control their emotions. Sally could have opted to take a moment by herself to calm down before actually doing anything about the actions of her mother-in-law and the stew. Instead, she just reacted emotionally.

Beth sent me her photograph for a career/personality assessment. I noticed she had the Intense Feelings and Emotions trait, and I explained to her that she probably inherited it from her father. She had told me that she hated her father for the way he verbally lashed out at her. She did not want to see him again. I said, "You know what it's like to be on the receiving end of such abuse." Now Beth could understand how her father must have felt when she exploded at him, which she also had a tendency to do so. She forgave her father, and she made amends with him before he died. She felt at peace with herself.

The Intense Feelings and Emotions trait appears to be more male-dominant, and the physical feature that indicates it usually appears on the right hand, occasionally on the left hand, and sometimes on both. I met a man who had this trait on both hands. His thumbs came up to the knuckle on his index fingers. The resulting behavior caused problems in all of his marriages.

This trait does have a positive side: These people come to the rescue when danger threatens another person. We hear about the great feats of individuals who, for example, lift cars off people who have been pinned down in an accident. This kind of energy erupts from people with the Intense Feelings and Emotions trait.

Channel the energy of the Intense Feelings and Emotions trait with exercise—work out at a gym, cycle, play a sport that requires physical stamina, or lift weights. One gentleman with this trait told me that when he exercised he felt more balanced and in control of his energy. When challenging situations confronted him, he found himself better able to handle them. If he found his anger about to erupt, he deliberately went for a walk to calm down.

Relationships

If you have the Intense Feelings and Emotions trait, and you find yourself about to explode at your partner, take yourself out of the room or create some space between yourself and your partner, until you feel less emotional. Find a way to calm down even if it means going out and taking a walk or jogging.

Children

Children must learn to understand and manage the Intense Feelings and Emotions trait. Parents need to help them find ways to defuse their anger before it gets them into trouble. If this trait is combined with Low Tolerance (close-set eyes) and Backward Balance (more head behind the ear as seen from the side profile), this trait cluster becomes an explosive situation waiting to happen, particularly if the children are raised in an abusive environment.

Sales

If your clients have this trait, they may suddenly explode at you in anger. Don't take it personally. Find ways to calm them down.

Careers

No careers correspond with this trait.

Philosophical

Interested in Philosophy
Gaps between the fingers

Around 3,000 BC, the Egyptians observed a strong correlation between the gaps between the fingers and the people's philosophical tendencies. When the palms are viewed with the fingers together against the light, you may be able to see a certain amount of space visible between the fingers. The larger the gaps or the amount of light you can see between the fingers, the more philosophical a person's tendency. Philosophical individuals continually search for answers on a spiritual and soul-searching level; the larger the gaps, the greater the search. They feel restless until they get a sense of balance and fulfillment. Additionally, Philosophical individuals have an innate sense of spiritual values, and they seek a purpose beyond material levels. These people may go on a lifelong personal quest to seek a lifestyle that gives them deeper meaning and satisfaction.

Many individuals who have the Philosophical trait surround themselves with stacks of philosophy books. They study at length to find the knowledge to further their inner journey. In some instances, they may go as far as traveling to India to study under a guru to find the answers they seek. They may even retreat to a monastery. Individuals who have the Philosophical trait in combination with fine hair (Sensitive), close-set eyes (Low Tolerance), high forehead (Intellect), may become so caught up in their search that they lose sight of what is happening around them.

Many individuals who have the Philosophical trait look for their answers in alternative religions, such as Eastern philosophies or Native American Indian philosophy, where spiritual traditions are linked to the relationship with the spirit and the earth. One woman who had the Philosophical trait said she now uses art to address some of her philosophical questions, and she finds answers in her creations.

The Groove Garden is held once a month in Fairfax, just north of San Francisco. At this popular event, people can either listen to soft relaxing music in a meditation room, or they enjoy free-form dancing in an adjacent room. The softly lit rooms are draped with large parachutes, which add to the ambiance of the evening. It's a great place for people to escape from the usual bar scene. People who attend the event have a noticeable profile in common: They all have the Philosophical (gaps between the fingers) trait as well as the Sensitive (fine hair) trait and narrow faces (builds confidence through knowledge). Many a time I have said to someone who lives in Marin County, "I bet you go to the Groove Garden." Needless to say, they are quite amazed, and they wonder how I could possibly know their habits. Some profiles are easier to spot than others.

Relationships

No relationship applications exist for this trait.

Children

The Philosophical trait is not seen in children. The trait may be observed once they reach their teenage years.

Careers

Careers that are more philosophical in nature may be of interest to individuals. They may enjoy occupations such as the ministry or other philanthropic pursuits. Otherwise, the trait can be seen in all careers.

Sales

This trait has no applications in sales.

Solitude

Short Horizontal Line

The Hermit
Short headline

Some people just need some time by themselves. These "hermits" probably exhibit the physical attribute for the Solitude trait, or in palmistry, it is known as the hermit line—a horizontal line on the palm of the hands near the base of the fingers. The line usually ends just below the index finger. (Notice the short line in the sketch.) Individuals with this need for solitude, however, can be very social once they go out. That said, in relationships, their partners may feel cut out of their lives at times. Sometimes, people who have this trait want to be left alone to gather their thoughts.

Many people with the Solitude trait enjoy activities that give them the time they need to be alone. One of my clients mentioned that he loves to fly his model airplanes in a remote area with no one around. He enjoys having the space just to himself. A woman I know, Ann, likes to work in her herb garden because it gives her the time by herself that she craves.

Amanda was familiar with a high need for time out by herself. She found her need for people and her need for her own private space a dichotomy, which she had to come to terms with. This push-and-pull made it difficult to create balance in her life. One moment, she needed people around her, then suddenly, she did not want to interact with people at all, and she needed to escape into her own space by herself. When she reached a point of saturation, she often took off in the midst of a social event. This puzzled her friends who wanted her to stay. Amanda's need for solitude posed a challenge in relationships as well. When she wanted her boyfriends to leave, she wanted them to go "right now." This behavior tended to confuse them, and they felt rejected.

Amanda wasn't surprised at these men's reactions. Her extremes left her feeling confused as well; at times, Amanda thought she was crazy. She started to see a therapist, but she still did not find the answers. When I explained the Solitude trait to her, she felt as if a weight had lifted off her shoulders. Her behavior finally made sense, and the internal struggle with her conflicting desires lessened. If she subsequently developed an awareness of the push and pull of her traits, she could actually change her behavior. Knowing why she behaved as she did, however, helped her better understand herself.

Another client of mine who had the Solitude trait told me that if she didn't have some time and space to herself, she felt claustrophobic and overwhelmed. Being by herself gave her a chance to replenish and renew herself. She placed high emphasis on needing time to be alone.

Relationships
If you or your partner has the Solitude trait and needs some time out to be by yourselves, neither should interpret this as being shutout nor not wanted. The person with this trait just needs time to gather his or her thoughts.

Children
Children with the above trait may disappear into their rooms or to a secret place in the garden just to be by themselves. As parents, you need to respect their space and their need to be alone. If the children spend too much time alone, however, you have cause for concern.

Sales
This trait has no applications in sales.

Careers
This trait has no applications for careers.

Chapter Fifteen

The Legs

Short Legs (long waist)
Built to be on their feet

Long Legs (short waist)
Can sit for long periods of time

Jennifer's desk job often created an issue in her life. She needed to be up and moving around, rather than sitting in a chair all day. There came a point during her work day when she couldn't stand being at her desk any more, and her mind stopped functioning—especially if she had to write up a tedious report. She found that going for a walk helped relieved the irritation of sitting for so long. If she didn't do this, she found numerous mistakes in her reports. Just stepping outside for a moment helped her concentrate better. Jennifer had short legs.

Jennifer could never understand how the person in the office next to hers, a woman with long beautiful legs, could sit at her desk for hours on end without complaint. Sometimes, she didn't even get up at lunch time but worked straight through.

The next time someone says to you, "I hate my desk job," check out the length of their legs.

Long vs. Short Legs

To determine your own leg proportion, stand in front of a mirror and see if your legs are longer than the upper torso of your body. If you examine another person, notice if their upper torso is shorter or longer in proportion to the length of their legs. Simpler still, ask someone if they are short, medium, or long-legged.

Short Legs

Leg length has a direct bearing on career selection and ability in athletic activities. Short-legged people's low center of gravity makes movement easy. They tend to get restless easily, particularly if they have the Restless (long space from the base of chin to the base of nose) trait. Also, as mentioned, short-legged people have a hard time sitting at a desk job all day. Many of my short-legged clients have shared with me that for them to sit still for long periods, they must run, work out at a gym, or take a long walk before coming to work or during the lunch hour. This helps them get through their day. Sometimes, their love of a job overrides their need to move around. They frequently appear to adapt to the situation. However, after a while, these individuals find themselves getting irritable, and they may take their irritation out on family or friends; they seldom take it out on a coworker.

One short-legged person shared with me that running gave him time to himself that benefited him, his family, and his employer. Because of this exercise, his mind felt clearer, and his production increased at work.

Long Legs

Long-legged people are more structurally suited to sit for longer periods of time, and they even enjoy a desk job. When individuals with this trait also have Procrastination (head narrower at the back than the front) traits, they may be seen as couch potatoes. In truth, they're quite content to spend hours sitting in the same place.

If you are long-legged, and part of your job activity requires you to stand all day, if possible, find a seat and take short rest periods for your legs. When on a vacation, plan a mixture of touring and physical activity. If your travel companion is short-legged, work something out ahead of time so you can choose activities you both can enjoy.

Individuals with short—to medium-length legs find walking a good exercise for reducing stress. If possible, try to select an environment where you feel the most relaxed, such as by the water, out in open spaces, or in a wooded setting.

Relationships

During a weekend in Yosemite, some friends, my husband, and I decided to hike up Half Dome. We had hardly climbed a mile and a half when our friends decided they'd had enough, and they wanted to go back down. Disappointed in this turn of events, the next day we agreed to go our separate ways and meet later in the evening. Our friends took a bus tour, and we hiked up to Half Dome. Our friends have the long-legged trait, while my husband and I have the short-legged trait.

If couples do not share similar leg traits, they too can feel disappointed when certain activities are not mutually enjoyable. Find ways to reach a compromise; understand and reconcile to the fact that each person enjoys doing different things.

A study of professional athletes would probably find some similar facial features and leg lengths within any given sport—even within the positions played in a particular sport. I met a female professional soccer player who plays goalie for her team. I noticed that when I looked at her face, her eyelids were exposed (Low Analytical). This indicated that she liked to take action right away. After that observation, I started to look at other goalies. Many have that trait. People who enjoy participating in sports also tend to have the following traits: Competitive (head wider at the back compared with the front), Risk Taking (ring finger longer than index finger), and Restlessness (long space from base of chin to base of nose). This trait cluster is often seen in professional sports players.

Children

Children generally develop their physical proportions by the time they reach kindergarten. The child with a longer torso (and shorter legs), however, can be distinguished at birth. Parents should guide their children into activities designed for this body type.

In basketball, most of the players are long-legged, despite the fact that this seems opposed to the physical feature and its corresponding trait. For this reason, long-legged children and teenagers need to take more time out during the game to stay fresh and avoid the back problems they may experience later on in life.

Parents whose short-legged children also have wide-set eyes (High Tolerance) should consider encouraging them to play sports as soon as possible. This keeps them out of trouble. One woman I met who has this trait cluster said that during her early years at school, she was constantly in the principal's office for disrupting the class or for bad grades. When she reached junior high school and started playing sports, her grades improved immediately.

If teachers find children in their classes having a hard time focusing or sitting still, they should allow them to take a break and do some stretching exercises in the classroom. This helps relieve some of their restlessness.

Sales

This trait has no applications in sales.

Careers

Short-legged people enjoy jogging, gymnastics, hiking, tennis, soccer, football, gardening, aerobics, wrestling, or mountain climbing. Thus, they often choose careers in sales, construction, nursing, professional sports, athletic coaching, or the military. This would also include waiters or waitresses or any job that requires standing. If you have a desk job, just make sure you exercise either in the morning before you go to work or at lunch time. This will help clear your mind, and you'll be able to stay focused on what you are doing.

Long-legged people enjoy cycling, swimming, golf, dancing, volleyball, yoga, high jumping, pole vaulting, ice skating, or ice dancing, and they often choose careers as professional athletes in these areas. No career requires long legs, but people who have this trait might just be aware of the ones that require bending over to work on a project, which may cause some back problems.

Chapter Sixteen

Using What we've Learned

This final chapter summarizes what we've covered in the previous pages and shows how you can put your new understanding of facial and physical features or traits to use in the following areas of your life:

1. Understanding Children

2. Determining Relationship Compatibility and Relationship Challenges

3. Determining Appropriate Careers

4. The Sales Arena

Understanding Children

We need to be more aware of the strengths and challenges children inherit. Personology gives you another tool to help you immediately identify children's innate abilities as well as their more challenging traits. Parents and adults who work with children need to teach children how to work positively with their individual traits.

I also want to stress that parents need to listen to and support their children's dreams. Children's dreams may not constitute their parents' dreams *for* them, but they are *their* dreams. As I've mentioned previously, many people have shared with me that their parents did not approve of their chosen careers. Others tried the career suggested by their parents, but it never gave them deep satisfaction; it became merely a job. Later in life, they decided to make their dreams into realities.

We constantly read horror stories about children at risk. If we can better understand their traits and talents while they are young, we may be able to help them avoid some of the difficulties they go through later in life. Parents need this information about traits as much as their children do, for parents have inherited their traits from their parents as well. Parents need to work on their own challenges and to understand those of their partners and their children.

Here are some traits we need to be aware of in children along with some tips for parents:

Physical Feature	What It Indicates
Fine Hair	High Sensitive: Feelings are easily hurt. Tip: If children run off into their rooms or suddenly burst into tears due to a remark made, find out what has sparked their emotions or made them uncomfortable.
Coarse Hair	Low Sensitive: Loves the outdoors; may not appear as sensitive to others; tends to have a louder voice and enjoys loud music. Tip: If children appear insensitive toward others, explain to them how their actions affect people who are more sensitive.
Close-Set Eyes	Low Tolerance: Good with details; may focus on problems to the point where they get bigger than life. Tip: Check to see what troubles them; help these children look at the reality of situations. Be there to support them.
Wide-Set Eyes	High Tolerance: May get easily distracted in school. Tip: Make sure they don't have too many activities going on at once. Ask children for deadlines.
Narrow Face	Builds Confidence: Hesitant about getting into new situations, like the first day in a new school; may lack self-esteem, especially if peer groups or family members constantly put them down; keep in mind they build their confidence through knowledge. Be there to support them.

Tip: If they feel hesitant about a test or situation that causes some worry, don't just brush their fear off by saying, "Oh you'll do fine. Don't worry." Find out what is causing their anxiety; it may be nothing much or it could be a big issue for them.

Wide face

High Self-Confidence: Needs to be challenged or becomes easily bored; potential leaders.
Tip: Teach them to be sensitive to others; encourage such children to help fellow students who are less sure of themselves.

Outer Corner of Eye Lower than Inner Corner

The Perfectionist: Tries hard to do things perfectly to please parents; parent(s) will also have this trait.
Tip: First, praise these children for what they have done, before telling them what they can improve upon. Encourage them to look for the good in what others have done; be more sensitive to criticizing them for what was not done or mistakes made. Remember: Their performance does not have to be perfect every time. Don't put your expectations on your children, since this may set them up to fail or to develop a low opinion of themselves.

Vertical Forehead

Sequential Thinker: Step-by-step learner; exams may be challenging for them.

Tip: Encourage these children to ask questions if they do not fully understand what has been taught. When possible make sure they study well in advance; this takes the panic out of taking a test. Praise them for what they know. If students have a hard time during exams, suggest that they play music in their heads; this helps them relax. Don't rush or surprise them with last-minute changes in plans. They like to know about plans ahead of time.

Sloped Forehead

Objective Thinker: Mind works quickly; may not always get all the details.
Tip: Encourage children with this trait to think first before jumping to conclusions. Teach them to be patient with others who think and act more slowly.

More Head Behind Ear

Backward Balance: Has a tendency to hold on to negative situations and experiences.
Tip: Encourage them to let go of grudges or painful memories. Make sure you praise them. They may not ask for praise, yet they want it. They may enjoy anything that is historical in nature, such as art history, old buildings and collecting old coins or stamps.

More Head in Front of the Ear

Forward Balance: Loves to be recognized; may create the recognition they need by doing or saying things that have negative results, especially if they also have the Dramatic (flared eyebrow) trait.
Tip: Give them recognition and praise them for what they accomplished. Don't make them ask for acknowledgment; beat them to it, or they may "act up" just to get attention.

Long Thumb	Intense Feelings and Emotions: Both anger and emotions come quickly to the surface.
	Tip: Don't let children get away with expressing explosive emotions; explain how doing so affects others around them. Suggest that if they feel angry, they should engage in an activity where they can unwind.
Head Wider at the Back	Competitive: Loves competing; it's all about winning, it is extremely important to them.
	Tip: Sign these children up for a sport or activity into which they can channel their competitive drive. Teach them to back off when they become overly aggressive toward others. Ask them how they would like it if others behaved in an aggressive manner toward them. Teach them to recognize and praise others for trying.
Rounded ear	Music Appreciation: The enjoyment of playing or listening to music or singing.
	Tip: Encourage them to play a musical instrument, sign them up for singing lessons, or enroll them in a children's choral group. Take them to a music store, and let them discover how instruments are played and sound. Let them pick the one to which they are most drawn. Rent the instrument first to see how they like it.

Trait Cluster: Short Legs (Restless) and Wide-Set Eyes (High Tolerance)

May have a hard time concentrating.

Tip: Get them to exercise. Involve them in group sports, cycling, skateboarding, gymnastics, dancing, or anything that helps balance their energy.

Determining Compatible Relationships

We look for certain traits in compatible relationships. Yet even the best relationships face some challenges, but knowing which traits make people more compatible increases a relationship's chances of success.

We all have strengths and challenges; it's what we decide to do about them that makes the difference. Just because two people have significant personality differences doesn't mean their relationship won't work. They just need to be aware of their traits and how they affect the other person.

Many couples whom I have worked with, wished they had commissioned a Compatibility Profile earlier in their marriages; they felt doing so, would have helped smooth out the rough patches they encountered over the years. Couples having challenges in their relationships tell me the information gained during their consultations completely turned around their relationships. Knowing their partner's traits helped them gain a better understanding of each other. They placed enough importance on their relationship to invest the time needed to work on understanding their traits. Exploring ways to work with them or to compromise to meet each other's needs. One woman said that after their profile, her husband changed in ways that helped his relationship with her and his children. She said he became "a gem to live with—no more erratic outbursts" and, for the first time in years, he took time out to be with his family.

Physical Feature	What It Indicates
Width of Face	High or Low Confidence: If the man has a narrow face (Low Confidence) and the woman a wide face (High Confidence), she will tend to dominate the relationship. If the couple's faces are similar in width, this provides a good balance. Tip: If you have the High Confidence trait, be there to support your narrow-faced partner; don't push them around.

Spacing of the Eyes	High or Low Tolerance: If the woman has the Low Tolerance (close-set eyes) trait and the man has the High Tolerance (wide-set eyes) trait, this could create an issue in the relationship because of the different manner in which each individual reacts to situations. Wide-set-eyed people see their close-set-eyed partners as overreacting. Low Tolerance partners get extremely annoyed with laid-back, do-it-later High Tolerance partners. They want it done *now*. Low Tolerance people come across as over reacting to situations. High Tolerance individuals over commit themselves, and they end up annoying their partners because they do not complete things on time.

Tip: If you have the High Tolerance trait and your Low Tolerance partner asks you to do something, do your best to get it done; this avoids getting snapped at. If you have the Low Tolerance trait, try not to snap at your partner or to get overly intense; take time out and relax. If you also have the Controlling (cupped-out ears) trait, turn this trait off around your partner and family, or you may push them away. Think how it would feel if someone were to try and control you.

Hair Texture	High or Low Sensitive: This represents one of the more challenging traits in relationships. If one partner has coarse hair and the other has fine hair, the coarse-haired person (Low Sensitive) sees the fine-haired individual (High Sensitive) as overly sensitive. Fine-haired people find their partners rough or coarse and insensitive to their needs. Partners with the High Sensitive trait get their feelings hurt easily.

Tip: The coarse-haired person (Low Sensitive) needs to be more considerate to his or her High Sensitive partner's feelings. The fine-haired individual needs to clear up any misunderstanding right away when his or her feelings become hurt.

Leg Length

A long-legged partner is best suited to a medium—to long-legged partner. A short-legged partner is best suited to a short—to medium-legged partner. This allows them to enjoy similar activities. Partners with very different leg length, such as one with very short and one with very long legs, will find themselves with extremely different interests when it comes to activities of all sorts.

Tip: If two people have extremely different leg lengths, they need to explore activities they both can enjoy.

Personality Traits that Pose Relationship Challenges

Long Ring Finger

Risk Taker: These people may take huge physical or financial risks; they love to risk everything.

Tip: If you have this trait, think first about how the risk you want to take could affect your relationship. Explain to your partner the benefits the risk will bring; this will help reassure your partner.

Outer Corner of Eye Lower

Perfectionist: People with this trait constantly see faults in what the other person does or doesn't do; they may come across as extremely critical of their partners. This trait causes more relationships to end than any other.

Tip: If you have this trait, look for the good first, and keep criticism out of all relationships. Remember to praise your partner. Don't criticize them. It can be devastating, and they will feel they can never please you.

Exposed Eyelids

Bottom line: People who have this trait constantly interrupt and finish off their partner's sentences; this could annoy their partners, who either will feel unheard or that what they say is unimportant.

Tip: If you have this trait, try not to cut your partner off; be patient, and when possible, listen to what they have to say.

Square Forehead	Construction: People with the Conservation trait, may feel neglected if their Construction partner constantly works many hours. Their job becomes their hobby, and they can become consumed with it to the point they neglect their partner and family. When this trait is seen in a woman, she will much prefer a career to staying at home.
	Tip: If you have this trait, make sure you keep a balance between work and play. Take time out to be with your partner and family. If your wife has this trait, understand that she may not enjoy being a "stay-at-home" mother.
Vertical Forehead	Sequential Thinker: These people appear slow to respond to their partners' questions, which could become annoying. They quickly feel irritated if they are running late for an appointment or to catch a plane; they like to arrive in plenty of time.
	Tip: If you decide to change your plans at the last minute, give your partner who has the Sequential Thinker trait time to change gears. Also, understand your partner's need to be at an event, appointment, or at the airport in plenty of time. This avoids the stress that could come up between you if you run late.
Objective Thinker	Sloped-Back Forehead: People with this trait get impatient at the slow response of their Sequential Thinker (vertical forehead) partners. They like to do things at the last minute, which puts pressure on the Sequential Thinker.
	Tip: If you are an Objective Thinker and your partner is slow to respond, be patient. If you are the Sequential Thinker in the relationship, speed up, your responses; realize your slow response may irritate your Objective Thinker partner.

Convex Nose	Administrative: These partners like to be the boss. They are aware of the cost of things, and they look for the best price. They get annoyed when they see their partners being frivolous with their money.
	Tip: If your partner has a problem with over spending, sit down together and plan a budget for non-essentials.
Ski Jump Nose	Ministrative: Money is unimportant to people who have this trait. They have a tendency to spend their last penny. This could pose a problem in a relationship, especially when the partner with this trait doesn't balance the checkbook.
	Tip: Sit down together or with your financial advisor, and work out a budget with which you both can live. Set aside some money just for spontaneous spending, and don't go beyond that budget.
Head Wider at the Back	Competitive: A High Competitive wife feels frustrated if her husband has the Low Competitive and the Low Progressive (head narrower at the back compared with the front) traits. The wife may hold great aspirations for herself (or for him), while the husband with the Low Competitive trait feels happy with life just as it is.
	Tip: If you have this trait, direct your competitiveness toward yourself. Don't pressure or nag your noncompetitive partner. If you are the procrastinator create a short list of the things your partner has asked you to do, and give yourself deadlines for accomplishing these tasks. This avoids the nagging your partner feels compelled to do. If you are the more aggressive and competitive half of the couple, acknowledge and express your appreciation when your partner completes projects.

Finding the Right Careers

Individuals change their careers as many as seven times during their lifetime. Actually, choosing a career poses a huge problem for many college students. According to some counselors, 70 percent of students leave universities or colleges still uncertain about what career to pursue. Many Stanford University graduate students have been referred to me because they remain lost in the career maze to such an extent that they begin to doubt their own judgment.

Using Face Pattern Recognition, so much of this uncertainty can be avoided. By studying a person's facial features, it becomes possible to recognize an individual's innate abilities and talents and the careers that would best suit or interest him or her.

The following provides a list of traits and the careers or jobs for which people with these innate abilities are best suited. The trait by itself does not indicate that someone has all the qualities required for a job profile; a complete career profile would be needed to see if a particular job represented a good match. To get the best career matching results, contact the e-mail address given at the end of the book. The Career and Personality Assessment Profile (CAPA Profile) can be accurately assessed from photographs or in person.

Physical Feature	What It Indicates
Low Outer Corner of Eye	Critical Perception Possible Career Choices: Text or film editing, construction, electrolysis, accounting, coaching sports, engineering, or any career that benefits from natural precision skills
Close-Set Eyes	Low Tolerance Possible Career Choices: Accounting, finance, nursing, dentistry, nutrition, court reporting, teaching, counseling, or anything else requiring attention to detail
Convex Nose	Administrative Possible Career Choices: Finance, management, lawyer, project management, investment management, or stockbroker.

Ski Jump Nose	Ministrative Possible Career Choices: Nursing, customer service, volunteering, social work, sales (if they have Competitive trait), preschool teaching, or reception
Rounded Eyebrow	Mechanical Appreciation Possible Career Choices: Event planning, professional organizing, flower arranging, engineering, resort management (if they also have the Administration and Conservation traits), human resource management, and project management (if they also have the Design and Conservation traits)
Inverted V Eyebrow	Designer Appreciation Possible Career Choices: Architecture, Web design, interior design, engineering, photography (if also have close-set eyes), business consulting, landscape architecture, event planning, or construction
Oval Forehead	Conservation Possible Career Choices: Health-related fields such as dentistry (if they have close-set eyes), chiropractic (if they have short to medium legs), counseling, coaching, teaching (if they have close-set eyes), as well as building contracting, hotel management (if they have a convex nose), or any job that requires managing projects
Square Chin	Pugnacity Possible Career Choices: Mediation, law, or volunteering for environmental or humanitarian causes

Flared Eyebrows	Drama
	Possible Career Choices: Acting, public speaking, sales training, teaching, or any career that benefits from a natural flair for drama and art
Head Wider at the Back	Competitive
	Possible Career Choices: Sales, marketing, politics, law enforcement, politics, executive corporate management, coaching sports, or any career that would benefit from this competitive nature
Pronounced Cheekbone	Adventurous
	Possible Career Choices: Travel agency, tour guiding, international marketing and sales (if they have the Adventurous and Competitive traits)

The above notes represent broad brushstrokes. To get an accurate career assessment, you need to either have a private consultation in person or, if you live too far away, from photographs.

The Sales Arena

As the old saying goes, "Nothing starts until something is sold." Another adage states, "We all are selling something." In other words, we all are trying to influence others for some reason or purpose. That means we all are salespeople on some level, whether we are "officially" labeled a "salesperson" or not. My comments here, however, focus on the formal selling process.

Today, with so much customer competition, salespeople need all the tools they can lay their hands on. Being able to instantly recognize your customers' preferred buying styles gives you the added edge. It helps avoid "turn offs" with your potential customers, and it can assist you in setting up an immediate rapport with them. For example, you will definitely need to produce the evidence first for Skeptical individuals, or you will lose them as your customers. When you do so, though, you increase your chances of making a sale.

When selling anything for any reason (yourself or a product or service), here are some of the key traits to look for in prospective clients to help you make the sale.

Physical Feature	What It Indicates
Convex Nose	Administrative Tip: With this bargain hunter, talk about the value of the service or product. If you have a special on this month, place an emphasis on the added value. Show these customers price comparisons so they know what a bargain they're getting.
Ski jump nose	Ministrative Tip: Talk about how the product will serve them; money is not as important an issue, unless they really have a tight budget. In many cases, this person will end up spending more than they intended, especially if their ears are laid back against their head (Low Acquisitive) trait. This indicates they will spend their last penny and then some.

Down-Turned Nose	The Skeptic

Down-Turned Nose

The Skeptic
Tip: Show these people the facts and all the information. They want the proof first, so be able to back up whatever you say with relevant details. If they also have the Critical (outer corner of eye lower than inner corner) trait, these individuals could be a hard sell. Just present them with facts, this helps overcome their skepticism. Remember, their motto is: "Prove it to me."

Fine Hair

Sensitive
Tip: Talk about the quality of the product or service. If it's noisy in the location where you have chosen to meet, your client will have a hard time listening to you. So move to a quieter place. If you are a real estate agent, remember that clients with fine hair enjoy quieter locations.

Coarse Hair

Less Sensitive
Tip: If you have a soft voice, speak up with a firm voice.

Narrow Face

Build Confidence Through Knowledge
Tip: Clear up any questions these people may have, and make sure they fully understand how to use the product or service you are selling. Talk about the support program your company offers should they need help once they have purchased the product. If what you are selling them constitutes something new to them, expect some uncertainty.

Vertical Forehead	Sequential Thinker

Vertical Forehead — **Sequential Thinker**

Tip: Use a step-by-step approach; do not rush these people into buying anything, or you'll lose them as a client. Check that they fully understand the product or service. Keep checking in to see that your presentation has been clear so far. Give them some time to think over what you have told them. Be prepared to review the information again with them, if necessary. Ask them if they need to think about the product, service, or presentation for a while; this takes the pressure off them and helps them reach a decision more easily.

Exposed Eyelids — **Low Analytical**

Tip: Don't get too detailed with these people, unless they need the information. They prefer that you simply get to the point. Watch for signals that they've understood and want to buy now. That's your cue to stop and close the deal.

Thin Lips — **Concise**

Tip: Be concise and to the point with your sales presentation; don't go on and on, or they'll get bored and turn off the conversation.

Height of Eyebrow — **High Selective**

Tip: If the eyebrows are high-set (High Selective), allow yourself some time to get to know this person before trying to sell them something. Do not appear too casual or move into their space too quickly. If you notice they are stepping away, it may indicate you are physically too close for their comfort. Give them time to make a decision, or preface your final words by saying, "Do you need to give this some more thought?" or, "Is there something you are not clear on yet?" If the client's eyebrow are low-set (Friendly), feel free to adopt a more casual and friendly approach.

Chapter Seventeen

Trait Clusters

When some traits are combined with others in what I call "clusters," they can produce some interesting dynamics. I've mentioned a few of these in earlier chapters. You'll find them repeated here along with a few more.

Low Tolerance   Very Sensitive   Emotional

1. When individuals have large irises (High Emotional Expression), fine hair (High Sensitive) and close-set eyes (Low Tolerance), they can experience intense emotions. People with this trait combination feel other people's sadness at a deep level, even though they do not personally know the individuals involved in tragedies. They are greatly moved by what happens around them.

High Emotions   Ministrative   Generous

2. The jurors' levels of emotions play an important role in the courtroom when it comes to winning or losing a case, particularly if there is an abuse or personal injury issue at stake. Jurors feel extremely moved emotionally by cases related to either physical or emotional abuse. Therefore, they have greater sympathy for the victim. Jurors certainly will be on the side of the victim if they have ski jump noses (High Ministrative) and full lower lips (Generous). The money awarded will more likely be greater than it would be from a jury of people with thin lips and convex nose.

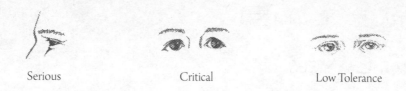

Serious   Critical   Low Tolerance

3. A deep-set-eyed (Serious) individual can really take the fun out of life, particularly if a person with this trait also has the outer corner of eyes lower than the inner corner (High Critical) and close-set eyes (Low Tolerance).

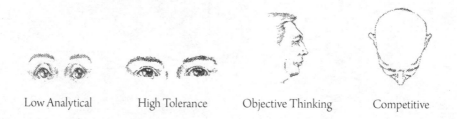

Low Analytical   High Tolerance   Objective Thinking   Competitive

4. Individuals with exposed eyelids (Low Analytical), wide-set eyes (High Tolerance), sloped-back forehead (High Objective Thinking), and wider head at the back compared with the front (High Competitive) often leap before they look. They make decisions before all the information has been presented to them. They want to know the benefits rather than go into all the details. They are more action driven—come on, let's go.

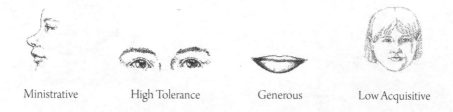

Ministrative   High Tolerance   Generous   Low Acquisitive

5. When individuals have a combination of ski jump nose (Ministrative) with wide-set eyes (High Tolerance), full lower lip (High Generous) and ears flat against the head (Low Acquisitive), they may find themselves spending their last penny and then some. This person could easily be taken advantage of due to their over-willingness to share what they have. They have an overly generous nature.

Administrative: convex nose

Acquisitive: Cupped-out Ears

6. Thin lower lip (tight with money), convex nose (Administrative) and cupped-out ears (High Acquisitive) individuals hang on to their last penny. To others, they appear stingy or tight with their money. They will not spend more than they must, unless it is for themselves.

High Self-Confidence

Administrative

7. People with a wide-face (High Self-Confidence) and a convex nose (High Administrative) definitely like to be in charge. They enjoy finance-related careers, although the traits do not guarantee success.

High Authoritative

Administrative

Competitive

8. A trait combination of wide jaw (High Authoritative), a convex nose (High Administrative), and Competitive (head wider at the back) makes these people feel it is their "right" to lead. They blaze a trail for others to follow, and they inspire others with their knowledge and courage. However, when something is not handled correctly, they

take the task away and do it themselves, rather than explain how they want it to be done.

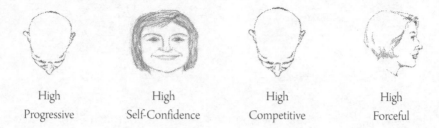

<table>
<tr><td>High
Progressive</td><td>High
Self-Confidence</td><td>High
Competitive</td><td>High
Forceful</td></tr>
</table>

9. When the head is wider at the back (High Progressive) trait is combined with wide face (High Self-Confidence), head wider at the back (High Competitive), and the head higher at the back compared with the front (Forceful), this trait cluster creates a force with which to be reckoned. These people are the movers and shakers and don't stand still for anyone. They like to be where the action is.

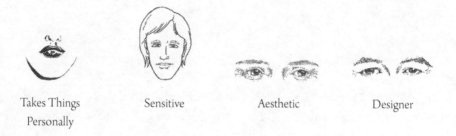

<table>
<tr><td>Takes Things
Personally</td><td>Sensitive</td><td>Aesthetic</td><td>Designer</td></tr>
</table>

10. The following trait cluster of Taking Things Personally (short philtrum) is a combination of fine hair (Sensitive), straight eyebrow (Aesthetic Appreciation), and an inverted V at the top of the eyebrow (Designer). This individual may enjoy a career as—a clothing designer, interior decorator, Web site designer, event planner, or may like any other design-related activity.

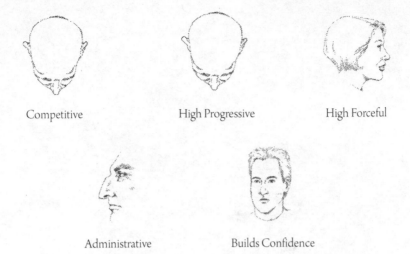

Competitive   High Progressive   High Forceful

Administrative   Builds Confidence

11. If individuals are Competitive (head wider at the back), Progressive (head wider at the back), Forceful (head higher at the back), Administrative (convex nose), and have a narrow face (Builds Confidence Through Knowledge), they may have self-doubts, but to others they appear dynamic. Often, friends or coworkers are amazed to learn these people are intimidated by new challenges. The energy of individuals with this trait cluster moves them into challenging situations. Their energy feels magnetic; people become inspired by them.

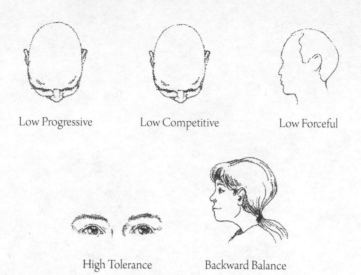

Low Progressive   Low Competitive   Low Forceful

High Tolerance   Backward Balance

12. A trait combination of Low Progressive (head narrower at the back), Low Competitive (head narrower at the back), head lower at the back (Low Forceful), High Tolerance (wide-set eyes), and more head behind the ear compared with the front Backward Balance (more head behind the ear) creates dreamers. They think a lot about doing things, but they may never do anything to make their ideas come to fruition. Create a short list of three things to do. Set deadlines throughout the day and short term goals.

Conclusion

There you have it! Hopefully this book has helped shed some light on how each of our differences makes us unique individuals and on how we might better understand ourselves and one another—and even get along better. No two people are exactly the same, but we are similar in some ways. As best-selling author Margaret J. Wheatley writes in her book *Turning to One Another: Simple Conversations to Restore Hope to the Future*, "It isn't differences that divide us. It's our judgments about each other." All journeys have a starting point. By understanding our differences and appreciating them, we allow better relationships, more enjoyable careers, healthier parenting, and greater self-fulfillment.

To not know who we are is to be lost. Face Pattern Recognition helps answer the big questions: "Who am I Who are You?" "What is my purpose?" and "Where am I going?" It provides a map for us to reconnect with our internal GPS or compass. The ability to identify facial features and their corresponding personality characteristics helps us get back on track with our lives so we move in the direction we desire. I invite you to start your journey today.

Glossary of Traits

Acquisitive	The need to acquire possessions
Adventurous	To explore new places or interests
Administrative	To administrate/oversee
Affable	Very friendly
Analytical	To analyze
Aesthetic appreciation	An appreciation of balance and harmony
Authoritative	Naturally authoritative
Automatic giving	Generous nature
Automatic resistance	To be stubborn
Backward balance	Relate to what has happened in the past
Body balance	Built to sit or stand
Competitive	The love of competing with oneself or others
Conciseness	Brevity of expression
Conservation	To maintain and look after
Construction	Enjoys starting and developing new projects
Credulity	To be open to new ideas, has a trusting nature

Critical	To be critical and notices the errors
Design appreciation	The appreciation of how something is designed
Discriminative	To be selective and more formal
Dry wit	Has a dry sense of humor, can be sarcastic
Emotions	The depth of feelings expressed and felt
Forward balance	Think in terms of the future rather than the past
Growing trend	Interested in all aspects of growth
Hand dexterity	The ability to work with the hands
The idealist	High standards
Imagination	To imagine things in one's mind
Impulsive	To respond instinctively, verbally, and physically
Innate self-confidence	Builds confidence through knowledge
Magnetism	The magnetic sparkle in the eye
Ministrative	To spontaneously serve people
Mood swings	Changing from one mood to another
Music appreciation	A high appreciation of music

Objective thinking	The timing of the mental response to situations
Organizer	To organize
Pessimism	To be negative about life in general
Philosophical	Strong philosophical interests
Physical insulation	Sensitive to sound, taste, touch, and feelings
Pioneer	To explore new concepts and new territory
Progressive	To take ideas forward
Pugnacity	To debate to fight for what you believe in
Restless	A need to be on the go
Seriousness	Takes the world on their shoulders
Sharpness	To investigate
Risk taker	The enjoyment of high risks
Takes things personally	Sensitive to criticism
Talkative	A need to embellish conversation
Tenacious	To stick with something to the end
Tolerance	Timing of the emotional response to situations
Unconventional	An unconventional approach

Index of Features

ABOUT THE AUTHOR

Naomi Tickle is a world-renowned Face Pattern Recognition expert and career consultant. As the president of Face Language International, she was responsible for developing the Career and Personality Assessment (CAPA) Profile. She has designed a series of face reading card decks for sales and relationships, as well as a master deck for multiple uses. She teaches workshops and lectures to audiences worldwide.

Naomi has been a guest on BBC, CNN, NBC, *Good Morning America*, and numerous radio shows. She has been featured in *Cosmopolitan*, the *Los Angeles Times*, the *Sunday Times*, and many other major magazines and newspapers. She has led workshops at Norwich University, IBM marketing divisions, National Semiconductor, CNN, AT&T, the World Trade Center, and college and dental conferences, as well as for many other organizations.

Additionally, Naomi has worked with hundreds of people who are in career transition. She helps students decide on their college majors and works with people who simply want to improve the quality of their lives. As one client put it, "Naomi teaches us how to know ourselves and provides an incredible opportunity to create a powerful change in our lives."

Through her work, Naomi has a threefold goal: to help people of all ages reach their full potential; to help them gain a better understanding of themselves and their family, friends, and business associates; and to make a difference.

Services and Contact Information

Lectures / Workshops

Naomi offers entertaining and informative workshops and lectures throughout the United States, Canada, Australia, and Europe. Attendees leave with the knowledge of how to use Face Pattern Recognition in their businesses and in their personal lives. The information offered provides a great tool for sales, teaching, coaching, team building, communications, personal development, as well as in meeting new clients for the first time or in any situation where you interact with people on a daily basis. To book a workshop for your conference or event, see the contact information at the end of the book.

> *I want to thank you very much for your workshop at the conference. It was a really refreshing part of the event. It's still a real talking point two weeks afterward. Very few speakers have that effect! FAMA conference*

Career / Personality Assessment from Photographs

A personology assessment helps you get a clearer understanding of your strengths and challenges and ways to master them. This assessment will

- create a work/life balance that suits you,

- build self-confidence and self-esteem,

- identify the careers that match your innate abilities,

- improve communications and personal development, and

- help you better understand yourself, your partner, and the people with whom you work.

> *I just got your report. What a fantastic thing! The boiled-down part about careers, avocations, and hobbies was exactly on target. I really enjoyed the process. Thanks so very much. Kathryn P., PhD*

Card Decks

Naomi Tickle has designed a unique set of cards that are convenient to carry in your pocket for easy reference. Each deck has a sketch on one side and a brief description of the trait on the other side. These provide a great tool for sales, meeting new clients, understanding your students, or simply finding out more about your friends and family.

The Sales Deck

This face reading deck features the traits that relate specifically to sales. A great tool that helps salespeople immediately identify clients' preferred buying style.

The Relationship Deck

This deck helps people learn how to identify the traits that create the greatest challenges in their relationships. When both people in a relationship have a better understanding of each other's traits, this helps avoid bumpy times in the relationship.

For further information or to order a card deck, please contact *Naomitickl@aol. com* or call 707-769-0290. You can also visit *www.thefacereader.com*.